Christmas 2021

Dear Sr. Ann,

I know that you love the Psalms as much as I do. Enjoy these meditations.

Much Love,
Kris

DAILY MEDITATIONS
ON THE PSALMS

*"The Lord is my shepherd;
there is nothing I shall lack.*—Ps 23:1

DAILY MEDITATIONS ON THE PSALMS

MINUTE MEDITATIONS FOR EVERY DAY CONTAINING A PSALM READING, A REFLECTION, AND A PRAYER

By
Rev. Msgr. C. Anthony Ziccardi

Illustrated

CATHOLIC BOOK PUBLISHING CORP.
New Jersey

CONTENTS

NIHIL OBSTAT: Rev. Msgr. James M. Cafone, M.A., S.T.D.
Censor Librorum

IMPRIMATUR: ✠ Most Rev. John J. Myers, J.C.D., D.D.
Archbishop of Newark

Psalm quotations are from *The Psalms*, New Catholic Version © 2004, 2002 by Catholic Book Publishing Corp., used by permission.

(T-189)

ISBN 978-1-941243-05-3

INTRODUCTION

*H*E said to them, "These are my words that I spoke to you while I was still with you, that everything written about me in the law of Moses and in the prophets and psalms must be fulfilled."
—Luke 24:44

Of all the books in the Old Testament, Christians are most familiar with and drawn to the Psalms. This is probably because of their widespread use in the liturgy. Or perhaps it is because Jesus taught and Christians have learned that the Psalms refer ultimately to Him. Or it could be because the Psalms are, like the rest of the Bible, God's word to us, and simultaneously our word to God, our response to Him, whenever we use them to pray.

God has given us in the Book of Psalms an abundance of ways to address and express ourselves to Him—and these time-honored prayers can be especially helpful when events leave us speechless. The Psalms comprise prayers, individual and collective, devotional and liturgical. They include prayers of thanksgiving and lament, entreaties for help and hymns of praise. They recount the past, look forward to the future, and summon us to be present to the moment—in all its joy or pain, frustration or elation.

The Psalms dilate the heart with the breadth of human emotion. They sharpen the mind by imparting instruction and insight and wisdom. They strengthen the will by applauding the merits of virtue and faith, hope, and love.

There are many ways to appreciate the Psalms —historical, literary, theological—and all of them are useful. These ways are, however, not mutually exclusive. And every reading of the Psalms incorporates elements from each of these approaches. But the approach taken in this book is devotional. This is to say that it is personal and reflective. It aims to discern how particular verses of this psalm or another may speak to the experience of the individual Christian believer today.

The meditations offered here are theologically grounded and informed, but they are not intended to explain or teach theology. Rather, they are aimed at eliciting the reader's personal, reflective, and prayerful response. Often they will refer to the psalm verse(s) fulfillment in Christ or the Church. Frequently, they will point to how we should live as Christians. Always, they are intended to inspire greater faith and deeper prayer. Although brief, they are not pills to be popped, but candies to be savored. So give yourself a 5-minute break each day to pray and enjoy!

28 August 2014
Memorial of St. Augustine of Hippo

GOD, be gracious to us and bless us **JAN.** and let your face shine upon us. Then your ways will be known on earth and your salvation among all nations. **1**

—Ps 67:2-3

REFLECTION. At the beginning of a new year, we ask God to be generous to us because we are conscious that without His blessing even our best efforts will be fruitless.

We do not ask God's blessing only for our own benefit, but so that those who see how God cares for His people may be motivated to get to know Him and His ways and be helped by Him.

PRAYER. *Lord God, smile upon us, in order that we may reflect the light of Your face to others.*

 WILL abide in your tent forever and find **JAN.** refuge in the shelter of your wings. **2**

—Ps 61:5

REFLECTION. A tent exists in order to shelter those who enter it.

We can abide in God's tent forever by remaining in Jesus, that is, by now being members of the Church of which He Himself is the head. There we find shelter from all that would endanger our eternal salvation.

PRAYER. *Lord Jesus, You came to gather God's children under Your wings. Help us to respond wholeheartedly to Your call to remain with You.*

LORY in his holy name; let the hearts of those who seek the Lord exult.

—Ps 105:3

JAN. 3

REFLECTION. We are bidden to exult in the Lord because by the Son's Incarnation God has come to seek us who could not find Him.

Moreover, we are encouraged to glory in His Holy Name, which is none other than "Jesus," meaning "the Lord saves." Jesus saves us from our sins and finally from death.

PRAYER. *O God, as I rejoice in the gift of Jesus, embolden me to speak of Him to others and so glorify You in the world.*

 Y HEART says of you, "Seek his face." It is your face, O Lord, that I seek.

—Ps 27:8

JAN. 4

REFLECTION. The invisible God showed His face in Jesus. No longer visible now to our eyes, our minds can glimpse the outlines of Jesus' face in the Bible, the teaching of the Church, and especially the saints.

Keeping company with the saintly people of our own place and time, we can learn to perceive Jesus even in the least of His brothers and sisters.

PRAYER. *Lord, help me to seek to know You better every day through the Church and the neediest among us.*

THE Lord is good. His kindness endures forever, and his faithfulness is constant to all generations.

—Ps 100:5

JAN. 5

REFLECTION. Nathanael asked, "Can anything good come from Nazareth?" Yes, indeed, the Lord Himself Who alone is truly good!

But because He is not indulgent, the Lord's goodness may not always be blatantly obvious. Yet, He is always so. Once we have experienced the Lord's goodness, we should rid ourselves of all that is not worthy of His love for us.

PRAYER. *Lord, help me to believe in Your goodness even in painful situations.*

ALL kings will pay him homage, and all nations will serve him.

—Ps 72:11

JAN. 6

REFLECTION. When God disclosed the Messiah's birth to the pagan magi, they came bearing lavish, regal gifts and bowed down in homage before Him as to a king.

This event anticipates the future fulfillment of this psalm when Jesus will be acknowledged as King of kings and when the rulers of the earth will bring their treasures to the new Jerusalem. If we are residents there, Jesus will share these treasures with us.

PRAYER. *Almighty God, may the manifestation of Your divine love in Jesus move all rulers to serve Him by promoting justice and peace.*

WILL give you the nations as your inheritance and the ends of the earth as your possession. —Ps 2:8b

REFLECTION. God promised to the Messiah kingship not just over Israel but over all nations. Because Jesus' royal inheritance is universal, disciples from among the Gentiles also belong to Him.

Through Jesus, we ourselves have an inheritance, a share with all the saints in His kingdom, but only if we truly belong to Him. Do we belong first of all to Jesus?

PRAYER. *Lord Jesus, I belong to many people, but help me to belong to You first of all.*

 E WILL be filled with the good things of your house. . . . —Ps 65:5

REFLECTION. Promising that the hungry would be fully satisfied in the age to come, Jesus already fed the hungry during His ministry.

This was fitting for the One Who at His birth was placed in a feeding trough in Bethlehem, that is, the "House of Bread." Jesus has been giving His people the Bread of Life throughout the ages.

PRAYER. *Heavenly Father, I thank You for filling me with the good things of Your house: the Body and Blood of Your Son.*

LORD, my God, you are indeed very great. You are clothed in majesty and splendor. . . . You have established your palace upon the waters.

JAN. 9

—Ps 104:1b, 3a

REFLECTION. When Jesus did miracles such as walking on the sea, He would assure His disciples that He was the same person they had known earlier and encourage them not to be afraid.

This was necessary because Jesus' characteristic approach was not one of strength but of weakness and gentleness. It was not Jesus' way to overpower others.

PRAYER. *O God, help me to be humble and gentle, utterly convinced that Your power is at full strength in weakness.*

 HE precepts of the Lord are right, causing the heart to rejoice. The commands of the Lord are clear, giving light to the eyes.

JAN. 10

—Ps 19:9

REFLECTION. God's commandments are like the directions accompanying the products we buy. As the instructions help us to use these products well, so also the commandments help us to function well.

Far from being oppressive, God's commandments are right and liberating. Indeed, Jesus revealed Himself as the one Who came to round out God's law given through Moses.

PRAYER. *O Jesus, with You at my side, lead me to discover that the yoke of Your commands is easy and Your burden light.*

THEY cried out to the Lord in their anguish. . . . He sent forth his word and healed them. —Ps 107:19a, 20a

REFLECTION. The Son or Word of God often healed merely by His word. Jesus continues to speak words of healing in the Sacraments of Anointing and Penance.

In anguish, do we cry out to God only after we have tried to get relief in every other way? As all healing is from God, we should ask His help even as we seek out relief from healing professionals.

PRAYER. *Lord Jesus, I praise You for the Sacraments. Help me to receive them with faith and gratitude.*

LET them praise his name with dancing and make music to him with tambourine and lyre, for the Lord takes delight in his people, and he crowns the humble with salvation. —Ps 149:3-4

REFLECTION. The Baptist compared Jesus to the groom whose shouts of joy over His bride caused John himself to rejoice. The community of Jesus' disciples, the Church, is Christ's bride.

The Lord Jesus takes delight in His people, and He brings us back to Himself when we wander from Him. Is Jesus' love not reason enough for us to rejoice always?

PRAYER. *O God, may Your love manifest in Jesus fill my soul with joy and my mouth with praise of You.*

HE voice of the Lord echoes over the waters. . . . The voice of the Lord is powerful. —Ps 29:3a, 4a

JAN. 13

REFLECTION. Thunder over the seas points to the Lord's power. His power was manifest also at Sinai as He thundered from heaven to reveal to His people the Ten Commandments.

A gentler sound came over the waters of the Jordan in order to reveal Jesus as God's Son. The Lord's voice sounded over the waters of our own Baptism, granting them the power to make us God's children.

PRAYER. *Almighty God, help me to recall that You made me Your child and to realize that You love me as such.*

 UT my people did not listen to my voice; Israel refused to obey me. So I abandoned them to their stubborn hearts and let them follow their own devices.
—Ps 81:12-13

JAN. 14

REFLECTION. To listen attentively is the essence of obedience. It is difficult because it requires our humility and trust.

It is odd that we expect God to be responsive to us when we put forward our requests, but we ourselves are not readily responsive to the Lord. Daily we disregard His commands. The consequences can be costly.

PRAYER. *Blessed Mary, by your example and prayers, may we become obedient to God.*

HE GIVES the snow like wool and scatters the frost like ashes. He hurls down his hail like crumbs; who can withstand his cold? —Ps 147:16-17

JAN.
15

REFLECTION. The bitter cold and snow ultimately come from God and serve His purposes. Spiritually, they show us that it is possible for us to become cold; our love for others may die, as may our commitment to God.

As we flee the outdoor cold by taking refuge at home, the warmth that we experience there shows us the difference that love makes in our relationships with God and others.

PRAYER. *Almighty God, may the snow and cold help us to dedicate ourselves to diffusing the warmth of love.*

I WILL proclaim the decree of the Lord. He said to me, "You are my son; this day I have begotten you." —Ps 2:7

JAN.
16

REFLECTION. These words, originally spoken by God to the kings whom He anointed to rule over Israel, met their fulfillment in Jesus.

When Jesus was baptized, God anointed Him with the Spirit and identified Him as His Son. Later God exalted Jesus to His heavenly throne by the Ascension.

PRAYER. *Father, may I live as Your child each day and so come to reign with Jesus forever.*

BLESS the Lord who offers me counsel; even during the night my heart instructs me.

JAN. 17

—Ps 16:7

REFLECTION. The Lord gives us counsel through His word, as He has done for the saints throughout history. St. Anthony of the Desert heard God's personal summons to him to become perfect by giving away all his possessions.

If we make God's word in the Bible our own, then it will be recalled when needed and provide us with wisdom and guidance.

PRAYER. *O God, I praise You for not remaining silent but for speaking. Help me to be silent that I might hear You.*

 LOVE the house where you dwell, O Lord, the place where your glory resides.

JAN. 18

—Ps 26:8

REFLECTION. To Israel God showed forth His glory in the Exodus. The Lord's glory rested on God's dwelling and accompanied Israel in the desert.

To everyone God manifested His glory in His Son Jesus. Through our union with Jesus, God's glory resides in us. O that I would shine forth with Christ's glory that others might come to believe in God through me!

PRAYER. *O Lord, I see Your glory in the Church, Your Body. May it shine forth also from me, in my words and my deeds.*

IT IS good to give thanks to the Lord, to sing praise to your name, O Most High, to proclaim your kindness in the morning and your faithfulness during the night.

—Ps 92:2-3

JAN.
19

REFLECTION. The thought of what we must accomplish each day may weigh upon us. And at the end of the day we may be physically and mentally exhausted.

We may not feel grateful, especially for difficult days. Our toil and our feelings notwithstanding, it is good to thank God in the morning and evening because He continues to give us life and opportunities and blessings.

PRAYER. *Almighty God, grant me an attitude of gratitude today and every day.*

PUT your trust in the Lord and do good, that you may dwell in the land and be secure. —Ps 37:3

JAN.
20

REFLECTION. We all crave security. The lives of God's biblical heroes give us no illusion that perfect security is attainable in this age.

Other means to security, such as money, influence, and connections, are less sure than God and faith in Him. If we would have the security He offers, we must put our trust in Him by keeping His commandments and doing good.

PRAYER. *O God, I thank You for Jesus Who teaches me to trust You even when other things would seem more reliable.*

ECAUSE my hands were pure, he has rewarded me. For I have kept the ways of the Lord and refused to turn away from my God. —Ps 18:21b-22

JAN.
21

REFLECTION. Adam and Eve could not keep their hands from sinning because in their hearts they desired to know or experience not only good but also evil. Doing evil things does not mature or develop us, but defile and distort us.

As Jesus was pure, we keep ourselves pure by recalling that we too are God's children and by keeping God's commandments.

PRAYER. *Lord, I thank You for Your commands. Help me to persevere in Your ways and to refuse to turn away from You.*

 EHOLD, children are a gift of the Lord, a reward of the fruit of the womb. —Ps 127:3

JAN.
22

REFLECTION. While the conception of any child depends on the sexual intercourse of a man and woman, their activity is insufficient to guarantee conception. Children are God's gift! Thus, their birth should not be prevented from occurring.

After birth and infancy and at every stage, children are God's gift to be welcomed and treated as Jesus Himself showed us.

PRAYER. *Lord Jesus, help me to welcome and embrace children, for to such as these belongs God's kingdom.*

E GUIDES the humble in what is right and teaches them the path to follow.

—Ps 25:9

REFLECTION. This life has a beginning and an end, as does a journey. Many are the paths which we might pursue on a journey, and the same might be said of life.

But only those who are open and humble can be led. Is it any wonder, then, that Jesus reached out to those who had already gotten lost and called fortunate the poor in spirit?

PRAYER. *Lord Jesus, You forged a path for each one of us. Help us to follow You in what is right.*

 HAVE spoken of your faithfulness and salvation. I have not concealed your kindness and your truth in the great assembly.

—Ps 40:11b

REFLECTION. The woman whom Jesus met at the well in Samaria told her neighbors about Him: how He knew exactly what she had done but did not reject her. They rushed out to meet Him.

Jesus, Who came to proclaim God's kingdom, would not want us to keep the Father or Him a secret. He sent His Apostles to make disciples everywhere. In turn, we too should become emissaries of Jesus announcing God by our words and deeds.

PRAYER. *O Lord, make us tireless emissaries so that the Gospel may be disseminated everywhere and sink deeper roots closer to home.*

LORIFY the Lord, all you nations; **JAN.** praise him, all you peoples.

—Ps 117:1 **25**

REFLECTION. Nations and peoples who were originally not part of God's people Israel were made God's people by Jesus through the ministry of the Apostles, especially St. Paul.

While only bishops are successors of the Apostles and enjoy their authority, all who have been brought into Jesus' fold should extend the invitation to others.

PRAYER. *O God, help me to invite those who do not know or believe in Jesus to join the Church, so that one day everywhere all may praise You.*

Y FOES taunt me, jeering at me all **JAN.** day long, "Where is your God?" Why are you so disheartened, O my **26** soul? . . . Place your hope in God.

—Ps 42:11-12a

REFLECTION. People may point to our hardships as evidence that either God does not love us or does not exist.

But Jesus Himself provides the response to such doubts; for the presence of sufferings in His own life did not mean that God had abandoned Him. The resurrection proved just the opposite.

PRAYER. *Father, grant me Your Spirit so that I may bear strong, loving, and wise testimony to You.*

ANY exclaim, "Who will show us better times! Let the light of your face shine on us, O Lord!"
—Ps 4:7

REFLECTION. Although we experience bad times, we sense in our bones that good times are normative. Goodness should obtain.

When times are not good, when we are in need, we rightly call out to God in prayer to smile upon us and grant us His help. As He wants to bless us, He will do so if it is for our ultimate good.

PRAYER. *O Lord, You are the source of every good thing in my life. I thank You from the bottom of my heart.*

 EFLECT on the Lord and his strength; seek his face continuously. —Ps 105:4

REFLECTION. We are always thinking. Sometimes our minds wander; sometimes they are focused on particular matters. But the matters about which we think may increase our anxiety.

Those who reflect often on the One Who ultimately matters gain perspective on everything else and their anxieties are quieted by God's strength.

PRAYER. *Lord, help me to turn my mind to You more frequently and to focus on You until the day I get to see You face to face.*

E IS like a tree planted near streams of water, which bears fruit in its season, and whose leaves never wither.

JAN. 29

—Ps 1:3

REFLECTION. All living things require sustenance. We need not only food and water, but above all God and a relationship with Him.

God nurtures us through His word in the Scriptures and His Sacraments which bestow His Spirit Who is life-giving water on us. Am I willing and eager to be nurtured?

PRAYER. *Almighty God, keep me deeply rooted in Christ and the life of the Church so that I may flourish and bear fruit that will endure.*

 WILL enter your house because of your great kindness, and I will bow down in your holy temple, filled with awe of you.

JAN. 30

—Ps 5:8

REFLECTION. "Members only" is posted in many locations and even on websites. Access is limited by human beings. God is desirous of the opposite as regards Himself and His house.

God gives access to Himself not on the basis of our merit, but His kindness. So He re-admits us often into His friendship by the Sacrament of Penance. And at every Mass, God enables us to have access to Him by the Penitential Act whereby we recall our venial sins and request mercy.

PRAYER. *O Lord, I thank You for the ability to be in Your presence and praise You.*

THEY have greatly oppressed me from my youth, but never have my enemies prevailed against me. —Ps 129:2

REFLECTION. Young people have many pressures on them, so that even when filled with many good things they may experience their lives as oppressive. Their suffering is sometimes caused or compounded by adults' neglect of them.

Rough behavior or carefree façades may be a clever cover for suffering. If we could see past these things into their hearts, we would support and defend them against harmful forces.

PRAYER. *O God, I thank You for helping me to weather the storms of my youth so that I can help today's young people.*

WHY, O Lord, do you stand far off? Why do you remain hidden in times of trouble? —Ps 10:1

REFLECTION. On overcast days, the sun is hidden by the clouds, but it continues to exist and warm the universe.

When we have troubles, we may doubt that God is present and active. But He is merely hidden from our view for a time.

PRAYER. *Loving God, when I am close to despair and think you have forgotten me, help me to believe that You are near and active nonetheless.*

IFT up your arches, O gates; rise up, you ancient portals so that the King of glory may enter. —Ps 24:7

REFLECTION. When the Ark was brought in, God's glory filled the Temple. When Mary and Joseph brought Jesus into the Temple, Simeon recognized and proclaimed His glory.

Jesus, the Lord of glory, was rejected and crucified. It is clear that His glory was not so overwhelmingly visible as to force recognition, but only to invite it.

PRAYER. *Lord Jesus, enlarge the portal of my heart so that Your glory may abide in me and radiate from me to others.*

OU are awesome and resplendent, more majestic than the everlasting mountains. —Ps 76:5

REFLECTION. Imagine snow-capped mountains. Is there anything more awe-inspiring? The sight of them alone is satisfying to some; yet, others are drawn to ski or climb them.

The Creator is more glorious than His creation. He is worthy of greater awe and exploration. We are truly blessed to behold Him and to call him Father.

PRAYER. *Father God, I thank You for Your creation which is a window onto Your awesome majesty.*

THE faithful in the land are the ones whom I will choose to be my companions. —Ps 101:6a

REFLECTION. Our parents taught us to choose our friends carefully because they can influence us for better or worse.

Like Jesus we should not shun people who do wrong but reach out to them with compassion. And like Him we should choose companions who are faithful to God and who can encourage us to holiness.

PRAYER. *Lord Jesus, grant me discernment that I may pick my friends wisely.*

THEIR own tongues will bring them down, and all who see them will wag their heads. —Ps 64:9

REFLECTION. Sometimes we are our own worst enemies. We end up being poorly treated by those we have offended; we are snubbed by those we haven't included in our activities.

When we boast about ourselves, we are likely to inflame others' jealous attempts to cut us down to size. Humility about ourselves and kindness toward others are the better course.

PRAYER. *O God, train my tongue to speak with humility and charity, and to ask forgiveness when I do otherwise.*

AY my prayer be like incense before you, the lifting up of my hands like the evening sacrifice. —Ps 141:2

REFLECTION. The psalmist does not have incense or a sacrificial animal to offer to God. He hopes that the Lord will accept as sufficient his prayer and his uplifted hands.

The best gifts that we can give to others are not necessarily those that cost a lot of money, but our time and attention and care.

PRAYER. *O Lord, make me truly generous in showing You and others my love.*

WILL not enter the house I live in or lie down on the bed where I sleep; neither will I allow myself to fall asleep or even to close my eyes, until I find a home for the Lord. —Ps 132:3-5a

REFLECTION. Many people are homeless, and many others tirelessly advocate and care for them.

Jesus Himself is homeless, unless we make room for Him in our hearts and lives. In the Book of Revelation, He says, "Behold, I stand at the door and knock."

PRAYER. *O Jesus, help me to welcome You more fully into my life as You continually invite me to share in Yours.*

YOU have kept count of my wanderings and stored my tears in your flask, recording all these in your book.

FEB. 8

—Ps 56:9

REFLECTION. Even if we don't have a degree in accounting, it is wise for us to keep track of our money, appointments, and accomplishments.

God too has a streak of the accountant in Him, but He takes note also of our tears and failures because He intends to compensate us for these in the future.

PRAYER. *O God, as You have counted even the hairs on my head, help me to be ever grateful for Your vigilant watch over me.*

———

 O LORD, let me know my end and the number of days left to me; show me how fleeting my life is.

FEB. 9

—Ps 39:5

REFLECTION. When time is limited, we prioritize and focus on what we should be doing.

If we remain aware that our time on earth is quite limited, with God's grace we will focus on doing what will make us saintly.

PRAYER. *Almighty God, help me to experience time, not as an enemy, but as a motivator.*

THE Lord looks down from heaven upon the entire human race.

—Ps 14:2a

FEB. 10

REFLECTION. Perspective depends upon the location from which one is looking. The world looks different from the top of a skyscraper or from the bottom of the Grand Canyon.

God views us and our lives from a superior vantage point. We can get God's perspective on the situations we face by prayer and reflecting on His word.

PRAYER. *Lord, help me to see the world and my own life from Your perspective.*

BLESSED is he who has concern for the weak; in time of trouble the Lord will deliver him. . . . The Lord will sustain him on his sickbed and bring him back to health.

—Ps 41:2, 4

FEB. 11

REFLECTION. Jesus characterized His mission as one of healing and Himself as a healer. Jesus' disciples cured the sick in His name.

As His greatest disciple, the Blessed Virgin Mary has secured innumerable healings from her Son. She has done so countless times especially at Lourdes.

PRAYER. *O Mary, St. John Paul II credited your intercession with the preservation of his life from deadly gunshot wounds. Intercede on behalf of all the sick, so that your Son may be glorified.*

I N GOD we boast the whole day long, and **FEB.**
we will praise your name forever.

—Ps 44:9 **12**

REFLECTION. Self-praise is an oft-recommended strategy to success. As God has more than enough success, He does not need our advertising. We boast of Him because He alone is completely worthy of praise.

We praise the Lord now and look forward to praising Him around His heavenly throne throughout eternity.

PRAYER. *O Lord, You are the basis of all my success; help me to praise You for all my accomplishments.*

T HE promises of the Lord are certain; **FEB.**
they are like silver refined in a furnace
and purified seven times. —Ps 12:7 **13**

REFLECTION. In the New Testament God brought to fulfillment everything He had promised in the Old Testament. What God has promised us through Jesus will also be accomplished in time. God's promises are sure.

They are also precious. What can compare to the promise of the Holy Spirit, the forgiveness of sins, the resurrection of the body, and life everlasting?

PRAYER. *O Lord, I rejoice in Your promises because You are completely truthful and reliable.*

MY Strength, I will sing your praises, for you, O God, are my fortress, the God who shows me love. —Ps 59:18 **FEB. 14**

REFLECTION. Many popular songs are about love. The one who loves expresses affection for the beloved in beautiful words. But sometimes romantic love does not go beyond words.

God, on the other hand, shows His love for us by His providence and mercy, by His gifts of Jesus and Holy Spirit and the Church. It is only right that we praise God and sing of His love.

PRAYER. *O God, may I see Your love more clearly and proclaim it more convincingly.*

 E CAUSES clouds to rise from the ends of the earth; he sends lightning with the rain and brings forth the wind from his storehouses. —Ps 135:7 **FEB. 15**

REFLECTION. Despite our ecological knowledge and technological savvy, we are hardly able to predict the weather—never mind control it! Severe weather conditions rightly humble us.

How great is the Lord Who created and set the elements in motion! If such wonders are in His hand, He could accomplish even greater things in our lives if we sought His help with humility and faith.

PRAYER. *Almighty God, let every storm remind me of Your great power and bring me to seek Your help.*

CREATE in me a clean heart, O God, and renew a resolute spirit within me. —Ps 51:12

FEB. 16

REFLECTION. Until addicted persons admit their need and seek help they cannot be healed. All who suffer from sin are in a similar position. Our hearts are defiled by ungodly desires and our spirits waver between choosing good and evil.

Lepers recognized that only Jesus could make them clean and He did. He still operates this way and waits patiently for us to seek Him.

PRAYER. *Lord, as You alone can help me overcome sinful habits, do not allow me to experience proud illusions, but hasten to my aid.*

 FOR you are not a God who delights in wickedness; evil cannot remain in your presence. —Ps 5:5

FEB. 17

REFLECTION. Evil is offensive to God, and He wants it to end. This is why God provided His law through Moses and His grace through Christ.

Evil cannot remain in God's presence because He overcomes it by His goodness and love. The ultimate proof is that God sent Jesus to invite sinners whom others had rejected as being beyond hope to repent and be saved.

PRAYER. *Loving Father, may I detest sin, but reach out to sinners.*

F YOU, O Lord, kept a record of our sins, O Lord, who could stand upright? But with you there is forgiveness. —Ps 130:3-4a

FEB. 18

REFLECTION. Life is not a game and God does not keep a scorecard. Otherwise, we would surely lose.

Although whatever we have done cannot be undone, God does not keep a record of our sins—as a bank might keep a record of our outstanding loans. Once forgiven, our sins no longer stand between us and God.

PRAYER. *O God, I marvel at Your readiness to forgive. May I seek Your forgiveness often especially through the Sacrament of Penance.*

 CALL upon you, O God, for you will answer me. Incline your ear to me and listen to my plea. —Ps 17:6

FEB. 19

REFLECTION. As the means of communication increase and multiply, the people we try to reach are often less reachable than previously. We are frequently leaving messages and waiting for a response.

None of this comes into play with God. He is eager to hear us; and He does so directly. Moreover, His responses are both more thoughtful and effective.

PRAYER. *Almighty God, You are always listening. Help me to be more prayerful.*

WHEN you do such things, can I remain silent? Do you think that I am like you? I will correct you and set the charge before your face.

FEB. 20

—Ps 50:21

REFLECTION. The Father sent the prophets to call His people to repentance, and Jesus urged His disciples to correct one another.

Minding one's business is an excuse for uncaring indifference when we stand idly by and watch others get ensnared by sin.

PRAYER. *Lord Jesus, like You, may I always speak the truth in love to those who are embroiled in sin.*

 IF I forget you, O Jerusalem, may my right hand fail me. —Ps 137:5

FEB. 21

REFLECTION. At times all of us forget this or that. But we do not forget what is really important. For example, we do not forget to eat because it is critical to our life.

Christians should never forget the goal of life: the new or heavenly Jerusalem. Otherwise, they may become sidetracked or go completely off the road. Sometimes serious failures can help us to realize our error and get us back on track.

PRAYER. *By Your grace, O Lord, may my failures help me to refocus on the ultimate goal of my life.*

FROM the ends of the earth, I call to you, with a heart that is fainting away; set me high upon a rock. —Ps 61:3

REFLECTION. While God Himself is the ultimate rock for His people, He is not alone; for by a special gift of the Father, Peter became the rock foundation of the Church.

As people from all the ends of the earth call upon God because their hearts are fainting, God's Church founded on the rock of Peter is there ready to receive and strengthen them.

PRAYER. *Father in heaven, move all Christians to be united in the Lord's service around St. Peter's successor, the Pope.*

THOUGH the Lord is exalted, he cares for the lowly. —Ps 138:6a

REFLECTION. Frequently the "high and mighty" are also proud. They think themselves better and more deserving than others. They cannot be bothered with the lowly.

The joyous irony is that the Most High God is also humble. He makes Himself the helper of all, especially of the most lowly. If we truly would be God's children, we too should care for those considered insignificant by the world.

PRAYER. *Almighty God, give me a spirit of humble service towards the lowly.*

PUT an end to the malice of the wicked but continue to sustain the righteous, O God of justice, you who search minds and hearts. **FEB. 24**

—Ps 7:10

REFLECTION. To diagnose and treat us, doctors often need to conduct special tests. God needs no such assistance since He Himself searches human minds and hearts.

He does so in order to diagnose and treat us spiritually: to rid us of malice and encourage us in righteousness. God communicates His diagnosis in prayer and heals us by the Sacraments.

PRAYER. *O Lord, may I take seriously what You show me about myself in prayer and avail myself of Your divine help.*

GIVE joy to the soul of your servant, for to you, O Lord, I lift up my soul. **FEB. 25**

—Ps 86:4

REFLECTION. Jesus said that He possessed joy in Himself, and that He wished that His disciples might be filled with His joy. God wants to give us joy, even through unlikely means.

Thus, lifting our souls to God in prayer, we should frequently seek joy from Him, rather than from those persons or things that can only provide us passing pleasure.

PRAYER. *O God, help me to stop chasing after passing pleasures in order to possess the enduring joy that You want to give me.*

OU were a forgiving God to them, but you punished their wrongdoings.

—Ps 99:8b

FEB. 26

REFLECTION. Forgiveness is not always or necessarily a write-off. Rather, it is the continuance of a relationship. Parents forgive their children, but simultaneously punish them so that they might learn to change their wrong behavior.

What true parents do not discipline the children they love? Because our heavenly Father loves us, He does not always withhold discipline.

PRAYER. *O Lord, let me see and accept Your love in the painful consequences of my sins.*

 E LED his people through the wilderness, for his love endures forever.

—Ps 136:16

FEB. 27

REFLECTION. God could have brought Israel to the Promised Land by many routes, but He chose the wilderness so that they might appreciate their dependence on Him, experience His providence, and learn to trust Him.

The wilderness was an expression of God's love for Israel. It is the same for us. When we feel lost in the wilderness, God is drawing us closer to Him.

PRAYER. *O God, may experiences of the wilderness become an opportunity for me to trust You more.*

THE poor will eat and be filled; those who seek the Lord will praise him.

—Ps 22:27a

REFLECTION. The poor eat and are filled when those who have more than enough share their food and resources with them. This is a major reason for giving alms and making donations, especially in Lent.

As givers we do not deserve praise because what we give belongs ultimately to God, and it is He who enables us to deny ourselves.

PRAYER. *Almighty God, help me to see the poor at my doorstep and to provide them with food and other necessities.*

BUT they soon forgot what he had done and had no confidence in his plan. In the wilderness they yielded to their cravings; in the wasteland they put God to the test.

—Ps 106:13-14

REFLECTION. Although God allows us to be in situations of great want so that we might turn to Him and experience His providence, we can easily lose faith and demand that God prove Himself in trying circumstances.

This can safely be avoided by our constant, deliberate remembrance of God's gracious deeds in the past towards His people.

PRAYER. *O God, revive in me the memory of Your past wonders and help me to hold in check my present cravings.*

EAR my voice in supplication as I plead for your help, as I lift up my hands toward your Most Holy Place. —Ps 28:2 **MAR. 1**

REFLECTION. As little children, we lift up our hands and arms to get the attention of adults who tower over us. We are confident that someone will respond, pick us up, and comfort us.

In the face of life's truly great difficulties, we are as limited as children. We can and should lift up our hands and voices to God to plead for His help for He is our loving Father.

PRAYER. *Father, I lift up my hands and my voice to You. Listen to me and respond lovingly.*

 HE Lord is gracious and merciful, slow to anger and abounding in kindness. The Lord is good to all, showing compassion to every creature. —Ps 145:8-9 **MAR. 2**

REFLECTION. The Lord is generous. He shows His kindness to both the good and the bad, as a father might do with his children.

Like the older son in Jesus' story of the Prodigal Son, we might perceive this as an injustice. The reality is that even good people need mercy, for there is no one who is perfectly good.

PRAYER. *Generous God, help me not to be stingy with my kindness by reserving it only for those I deem deserving.*

PUT on sackcloth and afflicted myself with **MAR.** fasting, while I poured forth prayers from my heart. —Ps 35:13b

3

REFLECTION. If we want God to meet some great need, we might show Him our earnestness by doing without a meal and soaking ourselves in prayer and supplication.

Jesus was no stranger to fasting and intense prayer. Can you and I afford to be so, as though we might be greater than He?

PRAYER. *Heavenly Father, help me to take Your Son as my model in earnest supplication.*

 S LONG as I remained silent, my **MAR.** body wasted away. . . . I said, "I will confess my offenses to the Lord," and you removed the guilt of my sin. —Ps 32:3a, 5b

4

REFLECTION. God knows our sins, and generally we are conscious of them too. This is not enough. We must own them and denounce them. Only then can we be free of them.

Admitting our sins to fellow Christians is helpful, but it is also necessary to confess them to a priest in order to receive sacramental absolution.

PRAYER. *Forgiving God, help me to make a thorough confession in the coming days.*

F ONLY my people would listen to me, if only Israel would walk in my ways.

—Ps 81:14

REFLECTION. At some time or other, we have all experienced the steep cost of not listening to our parents when they have given us advice or direction.

Not listening to God is as costly as, or more costly than, not listening to our parents. God wants to spare us this cost by inviting us to consider the rewards of obedience.

PRAYER. *Lord Jesus, help me to learn obedience to God from You.*

 EAR my prayer, O God; give ear to the words of my mouth.

—Ps 54:4

REFLECTION. While God insists that we listen to Him and what He has to say, we too can insist that He listen to us and what we have to say.

This is not being disrespectful, for Jesus assured us that God wants to hear from us because He is our Father. Indeed, Jesus encouraged His followers to be relentless in prayer.

PRAYER. *I praise You, Father, for giving us Jesus to show us how to relate to You.*

E IS mindful of his covenant forever, the promise he laid down for a thousand generations. —Ps 105:8

REFLECTION. A covenant is more than a contract by which two parties undertake respective duties to one another. A covenant is a personal bond between parties. God has made a covenant with us.

Covenants between human individuals, like marriage, often fail. But as God is perfectly faithful, He will not allow His covenant with us to fail.

PRAYER. *Lord God, make me mindful of Your covenant that I may remain faithful to it.*

 LEANSE me of my hidden faults. From willful sins preserve your servant; never let them gain power over me. Then I will be blameless. —Ps 19:13b-14a

REFLECTION. While we may be conscious of some of our sins, we may not be aware of all of them. Nevertheless, all sins do damage, as when a gadget breaks down from misuse.

God helps us to be rid of hidden faults as He brings them to our consciousness by His word and by prayer.

PRAYER. *O Lord, help me to identify my sins clearly and grant me Your grace to overcome them.*

BLESSED are those whose way is blameless, who walk in accord with the law of the Lord. —Ps 119:1

REFLECTION. To be blameless or free of sin brings God's blessings, just as being free of unhealthy foods contributes to our well-being.

Just as we may follow a healthy diet to maintain our body, we must follow God's law for the good of our soul. Hence, the need for us to be well versed in God's law!

PRAYER. *Almighty God, fill me with love for Your law and for You Who have provided it.*

I CRY out to the Lord with my plea. . . . Before him I pour out my complaint and tell my troubles in his presence. —Ps 142:2a, 3

REFLECTION. Jesus taught that if we have a grievance with another person we should first take it up with him or her, for to do otherwise would be to slight this person.

Similarly, when hardship comes our way, it is a slight to God when we bypass Him and grumble about it to people who may not be in a position to help us.

PRAYER. *O God, while the buck definitely stops with You, may I always approach You first of all when I have troubles.*

DO NOT hold against us the sins of our ancestors; let your mercy come quickly to meet us, for we are in desperate straits. —Ps 79:8

MAR.
11

REFLECTION. Sometimes it may feel as though God is punishing us for the mistakes and sins of prior generations. This is not God's way. Rather we are experiencing in our time the ripple effects of their failures.

In order for us to stop the ripples and to heal ourselves and future generations, we need God's merciful help.

PRAYER. *Almighty God, we cannot undo history, but by Your grace help us to move forward with hope into the future.*

 HE WHO offers a sacrifice of thanksgiving honors me; to him who follows my way I will show the salvation of God. —Ps 50:23

MAR.
12

REFLECTION. We make sacrifices and give up favorite things during Lent, but the sacrifice God desires most is thankfulness for our lives with all their blessings and difficulties because such gratitude bespeaks faith.

So too does being obedient to God's commands. Following God's way, shown to us most perfectly by Jesus, is sure evidence that we trust God.

PRAYER. *Almighty God, may my trust in You blossom into gratitude and obedience.*

I WILL bless the Lord at all times; his praise will be continually on my lips. —Ps 34:2

REFLECTION. Even on the night before He died, Jesus blessed God. The Lord is to be blessed or praised at all times because He works in all things for the good of those who love Him.

On sunny days and cloudy days, on days of gladness and days of sadness, the praise of God should be on our lips for sustaining us in this life and for preparing us for the bliss of eternal life.

PRAYER. *Lord God, help me to praise You sincerely in both weal and woe.*

HELP us, O God, our Savior, for the glory of your name; deliver us and wipe away our sins for your name's sake. —Ps 79:9

REFLECTION. Given the frequency or gravity of our sins it is not likely that we have earned or are deserving of God's help.

Love is the only reason that God helps us; and in doing so the Lord becomes known for His gratuitous and generous love.

PRAYER. *Almighty God, rescue me from the problems that engulf me, not because I am deserving, but because You are gracious and because others need to know this about You.*

KNOW that the Lord secures justice for the poor and upholds the cause of the needy.
—Ps 140:13

MAR. 15

REFLECTION. When hustlers succeed, cynics say that "God helps those who help themselves." But the psalmist declares that God helps those who cannot help themselves.

If we would be more like God, should we not cooperate with Him in helping the poor and the defenseless? Surely, God will help those who make common cause with Him by helping the poor.

PRAYER. *O God, as I pursue my own well-being, help me to reach out to the less fortunate.*

 E STILL and acknowledge that I am God.
—Ps 46:11a

MAR. 16

REFLECTION. Because we have mouths, we talk; because we have legs, we walk. We are constantly in motion and continually talking, as though everything would come to a crashing halt if we should stop.

Although our activity is important, truly critical is God's activity. It is beneficial, then, to stop frequently to contemplate Him and His actions.

PRAYER. *O Lord, I profess that You are God and I am not. Help me to recognize Your presence and to thank You.*

HE meadows are clothed with flocks, **MAR.** and the valleys are decked out with grain; in their joy they shout and sing together. —Ps 65:14

17

REFLECTION. In this beautiful scene, the meadows and valleys are there simply through God's activity, but the flocks and grain come from human productivity.

Since the Garden of Eden, God has called men and women to cooperate with Him in doing something beautiful. In what does God want to enlist my cooperation?

PRAYER. *Lord God, in my joy, I shout: thank You for calling me into life in order to collaborate with You and with others.*

 GOD, you know how foolish I am; **MAR.** my guilty deeds are not hidden from you. —Ps 69:6

18

REFLECTION. Some people think that sinning is acceptable, unless one gets caught. They believe that the point is to get away with as much as possible. This is all backwards.

To sin is to be foolish. Sin hurts not only others but those who do it. And whether or not others catch us doing it, our sins do not escape God's notice.

PRAYER. *O Lord, I praise You for showing me the path of wisdom, which is to do right and practice virtue.*

ENTRUST your cares to the Lord, and he will uphold you; he will never allow the righteous to waver. **MAR. 19** —Ps 55:23

REFLECTION. The cares of life are many, especially those of work and family. We can be tempted to lighten them by compromising our sense of what is right and just.

If we would remain righteous, that is, do God's will in difficult circumstances, we must seek His help. "Cast all your worries upon him, for he cares about you" (1 Pet 5:7).

PRAYER. *O God, like St. Joseph, the righteous man, help me to hold fast to Your will for me and grant me never to waver in doing it.*

BUT as for me, I nearly lost my balance; I was almost at the point of stumbling. **MAR. 20** —Ps 73:2

REFLECTION. Because human beings walk upright, unlike animals, we can easily stumble over obstacles that we do not notice on the ground in front of us.

As moral beings, we can also stumble and fall by choosing to do wrong things. The danger is ever present, and the risk of sinning can only be reduced by our vigilance and our attentiveness to God's word which exposes the dangers.

PRAYER. *Almighty God, I thank You for watching over me and for the many times You have preserved me from sin.*

IVE ear, my people, to my teaching; pay attention to the words of my mouth. —Ps 78:1

REFLECTION. Precisely because God has chosen us to accomplish a particular work, He firmly but gently guides us through Jesus and the Church. Because this teaching can keep us from making serious mistakes, it is a great grace.

At the same time, it is not an easy grace; for, before anything else, it requires us to set aside our own ideas and concerns and pay attention to God's word.

PRAYER. *Lord God, help me to make room in my mind and heart for Your word.*

NSWER me, O Lord, for your kindness is wonderful; in your great compassion turn toward me. —Ps 69:17

REFLECTION. What gets people to notice us? Beauty, accomplishments, and wealth! Others might look at us out of desire or envy. The psalmist appeals to God to turn toward him because of His compassion.

Following his example, we bring to the Lord not our talent and successes but our weakness and failures, so that He may answer us in His wonderful kindness.

PRAYER. *Father, turn toward me. Take notice of my failures and support me in my struggles.*

BEFORE I was afflicted I went astray, but now I observe your word. You are good, and what you do is good; teach me your decrees. **MAR.** **23** —Ps 119:67-68

REFLECTION. Suffering is a great teacher. When we suffer the consequences of our sins, we learn that moral principles and rules are not arbitrary but rational.

God's word is the light on our path, and He has provided it in His goodness. It is wise to study and observe God's word as it comes to us in the Bible and the teaching of the Church.

PRAYER. *O God, I thank You for finding me whenever I have strayed and returning me to the right path.*

LORD, your kindness extends to the heavens; your faithfulness, to the skies. **MAR.** **24** —Ps 36:6

REFLECTION. How great is God's kindness? It is limitless. It goes all the way to the Cross. How great is God's faithfulness? It endures throughout time for everyone.

We are the ones who restrict God's kindness and fidelity by our indifference and rejection.

PRAYER. *Loving God, reawaken in me the awareness of Your steadfast love and faithfulness so that I may be fully open to receive it.*

SACRIFICE and offering you did not desire, but you have made my ears receptive. . . . To do your will, O God, is my delight. —Ps 40:7a, 9a

MAR.
25

REFLECTION. As a poor maiden, the Blessed Virgin Mary would not have had the means to offer God the sacrifices described in the law of Moses; rather, she exhibited her devotion by embracing God's will.

She gave God's Son His humanity, and He offered it on the Cross in obedience to God's will. This was His loving sacrifice, and we have reaped the eternal benefits.

PRAYER. *Father, by the prayer He taught us, Jesus encouraged us to do Your will. Like our Mother Mary, may doing Your will be our delight.*

 HOW us your mercy, O Lord, show us your mercy. —Ps 123:3a

MAR.
26

REFLECTION. The mercy of God is not in doubt. He has demonstrated it abundantly throughout time, and He continues to display it even in our time to those who seek it.

We pray that God show His mercy also to us, primarily by His forgiveness, but also by filling our lives with blessings.

PRAYER. *Merciful Lord, look kindly on us who seek to follow You, and help us to show mercy to those who have lost their way.*

GOOD and upright is the Lord; therefore, he instructs sinners in his ways.
—Ps 25:8

REFLECTION. God does not abandon sinners to their sins, and He does not leave the lost to wander without direction. As a shepherd, God comes to recover the lost and to redirect them to the right path.

Since we have benefited from God's goodness, we too should seek out the lost and help them to find their way back.

PRAYER. *Father, I rejoice in Your instruction, and I praise You for Your goodness.*

MY GOD, my God, why have you for-
saken me? Why have you paid no
heed to my call for help, to my cries
of anguish? —Ps 22:2

REFLECTION. Jesus said, "The one who sent me is with me. He has not left me alone. . . ." The Son knew that the Father was with Him. But in His humanity, when He suffered, He did not feel God's presence.

Yet God heard Jesus' cries and helped Him, not by sparing Him death, but by granting Him eternal life. Let us be assured by Jesus that God will ultimately help those who cry out to Him.

PRAYER. *O Jesus, even when I suffer greatly, help me never to give up on prayer.*

YOU spread a table for me in the presence of my enemies. You anoint my head with oil; my cup overflows.

MAR. 29

—Ps 23:5

REFLECTION. Despite contrary forces and people, God blesses His faithful ones: sometimes materially and often spiritually.

Jesus said, "I came that they might have life and have it abundantly." For Jesus' disciples, God spreads the table of the Eucharist, and He anoints us with the Holy Spirit in Confirmation as He anointed Jesus for His mission.

PRAYER. *Lord God, in the midst of life's challenges, let me seize the abundance of Your grace, so that my inner self may be filled.*

 RESTORE us once again, O God, our Savior.

MAR. 30

—Ps 85:5a

REFLECTION. The Lord restored the people of Israel numerous times. Each time they recognized and repented of their sins, God came to their rescue and restored them to integrity and to friendship with Him.

Israel's story fills us with hope for ourselves and teaches us a lesson. God will restore us whenever we sincerely acknowledge our need—even our total collapse—and call out to Him.

PRAYER. *O God, our Savior, never tire of restoring us, for we are weak but You are strong.*

AVE me, my God, for the waters have risen to my neck. —Ps 69:2

REFLECTION. Sometimes our problems may be so complex that we begin to drown. As we cannot swim to safety in a mighty flood, so we cannot save ourselves when engulfed by overwhelming problems.

As Jesus called upon God and experienced His powerful salvation in the resurrection, we rightly call upon God Who can and desires to save us.

PRAYER. *Almighty God, when I am in danger, remind me to seek Your saving assistance.*

EAL for your house consumes me, and the insults directed at you fall on me. —Ps 69:10

REFLECTION. Unknown to Mary and Joseph, the young Jesus remained in the Temple to be in His Father's house; and later He expelled traders from the Temple to restore it to its prayerful purpose.

Jesus died because He was completely devoted to God and His house, not just the Temple, but all whom God was calling to Himself.

PRAYER. *O God, grant me to be as absorbed in Your affairs as was Jesus.*

BE GOOD to your servant so that I may live and keep your word. —Ps 119:17

REFLECTION. We need a purpose to live: our family, friends, vocation, or mission. The psalmist says that his purpose is to keep God's word.

The psalmist asks God to keep him alive for this worthy purpose. Whatever our purpose, it should be as noble; otherwise, it is not worthy of God or us.

PRAYER. *Almighty God, help me to conduct myself according to Your word and provide a positive example.*

THE misfortunes of the righteous man are many, but the Lord delivers him from all of them. —Ps 34:20

REFLECTION. In a world marred by sin, righteous people should expect not only to experience misfortunes but also mistreatment, as Abel was killed by Cain and Jesus by the Romans.

But God delivers the righteous "from all of them!" Knowing this, Jesus went willingly to the Cross. And we too can accept unjust treatment because He promised us eternal life.

PRAYER. *O Jesus, help me to endure ill treatment in the hope of final deliverance.*

YOU will show me the path to life; you will fill me with joy in your presence and everlasting delights at your right hand. —Ps 16:11

APR. 4

REFLECTION. Paths diverge. Some lead us to the desired destination, others not. By teaching them His will, God showed His people the path leading to life, not just temporal life, but eternal life.

The promise of "everlasting delights at your right hand" motivated Jesus to pursue God's will, despite the cost, and it is our motivation as well.

PRAYER. *Lord God, I thank You for showing me in Jesus the path to eternal life.*

 FOR the Lord is just and he loves righteous deeds; the upright will behold his face. —Ps 11:7

APR. 5

REFLECTION. While God allows human beings to sin and to be unjust, He wants all of us to be upright. Before Jesus, the upright could behold God's face symbolically by entering the Temple.

But when Jesus came, the just and unjust alike could see God's face. And Jesus Himself, the Upright One, would come to see the Father's face in heaven by the resurrection.

PRAYER. *O God, grant me to see You in others and to behold You in the beatific vision of heaven.*

LESS the Lord, O my soul, and do not forget all his benefits. He forgives all your sins and heals all your diseases. He redeems your life from the pit and crowns you with kindness and mercy.

—Ps 103:2-4

REFLECTION. How often God crowns us with kindness by forgiving our sins! How often He redeems us from the pit by sparing us deadly disease!

But even more wonderfully, God released Jesus from the grave and crowned Him with eternal life at His right hand. And because of Jesus, His faithful disciples can count on the same.

PRAYER. *Father, I praise You for Your goodness, which exceeds all bounds.*

 ITH God's help we will be victorious, for he will overwhelm our foes.

—Ps 108:14

REFLECTION. Victory matters in battle. It also matters in other areas of life. Victory over sin and death matters because these are everyone's ultimate foes.

God's Son Jesus knew that He could be victorious over both with the Father's help. With Him, we too can be victorious.

PRAYER. *Lord Jesus, grant me final victory with You.*

HE Lord is my light and my salvation; **APR.**
whom should I fear? The Lord is the
stronghold of my life; of whom should
I be afraid?   —Ps 27:1

8

REFLECTION. Fear is the appropriate response to whatever or whoever endangers our health and welfare. The reason for fear vanishes if God neutralizes such dangers.

Jesus was sure that God would defend and protect Him, so that He proceeded to the Cross in Jerusalem without fear, while His disciples followed Him in dread.

PRAYER. *O Jesus, help me to follow You fearlessly in doing God's will.*

N MY righteousness I will see your face; **APR.**
when I awaken, I will be blessed by
beholding you.   —Ps 17:15

9

REFLECTION. Jesus Christ, the only One Who was truly righteous, would be awakened from the sleep of death by the resurrection and see the face of the Father.

We who are made righteous by Jesus have the same sure hope. We too shall awaken from the sleep of death to see God's face for eternity.

PRAYER. *O Lord, I look forward to seeing Your face and the faces of my friends who have preceded me in death.*

LESSED be the Lord, day after day. . . . **APR.**
Our God is a God who saves; the Lord
God delivers from death. —Ps 68:20a, 21 **10**

REFLECTION. In the Old Testament God occupied Himself with the welfare of His faithful. Repeatedly, pious individuals and Israel as a whole escaped death with God's help.

The Father would save Jesus in a surprising and exceedingly wondrous manner by raising Him to a glorious life after His cruel execution.

PRAYER. *Almighty God, I bless You day after day for the sure hope of salvation You have given me through Jesus.*

UT I place my trust in you, O Lord. I say, **APR.**
"You are my God." My life is in your
hands. —Ps 31:15-16a **11**

REFLECTION. As young children, our life is literally in the hands of our parents. With these hands, they can nurture and protect us or hurt and destroy us.

God holds all of us in His gracious hands. Even if others hurt us, God will heal and restore us. Confident of this, Jesus went willingly to the Cross.

PRAYER. *Almighty God, through Jesus' death and resurrection, fill me with faith in Your love despite how others may treat me.*

BELIEVED; therefore, I said, "I am greatly afflicted."

—Ps 116:10

APR. 12

REFLECTION. When Zachary failed to believe the Archangel Gabriel, he was unable to speak. St. Paul shares the opposite result: because the Apostles had faith, they were able to speak.

It is because we believe in God that we speak to Him when we suffer. This is what Jesus did in the expectation that the Father would save Him.

PRAYER. *Father, fill me with faith in You that I might speak to You honestly about my sufferings and disappointments.*

OD will ransom me from the netherworld; he will take me to himself.

—Ps 49:16

APR. 13

REFLECTION. God would not only rescue Jesus from the shadowy dimension of the dead, but also take Him to Himself. Before dying, Jesus was confident that He was going to be with the Father.

God will also take Jesus' faithful disciples to Himself. If we believe this, the approach of death will not fill us with terror.

PRAYER. *Lord God, I thank You for revealing to us that death is the doorway into Your presence for Your faithful.*

N PEACE I lie down and sleep, for only with your help, O Lord, can I rest secure.
—Ps 4:9

REFLECTION. As Jesus handed over His Spirit to God, He said, "It is finished." He had completed the work God had given Him to do; therefore, He could let Himself fall asleep peacefully.

Not only did the dying Jesus experience a sense of completion but also security. He was certain that God would restore Him to a more glorious life.

PRAYER. *Lord, when I go to bed at night, may I sleep in contentment and security.*

 Y SOUL lies prostrate in the dust; revive me in accordance with your word.
—Ps 119:25

REFLECTION. Falling down in exhaustion is one thing, but being buried in the ground is another. Perking up again is one thing, but coming back to life from death is quite another.

From the Old Testament, Jesus received God's promise that the Messiah or Christ would be raised to new life after suffering death. He banked on this promise.

PRAYER. *Almighty God, I thank You for all Your promises, especially the promise of eternal life.*

EEPING may last throughout the night, but at daybreak there is rejoicing. —Ps 30:6b

APR.
16

REFLECTION. When Jesus died, the sun set on His disciples' lives. They mourned Him and the loss of their hope. And their mourning lasted until He rose from the dead.

Still weeping, Mary Magdalene and the other women came to the tomb at sunrise. When Mary saw Him alive, she ran back to tell the disciples the joyful news.

PRAYER. *Father, let every sunrise remind me of Your Son's resurrection and fill me with hope and joy.*

 WAITED patiently for the Lord; then he stooped down and heard my cry. He raised me up from the desolate pit. —Ps 40:2-3a

APR.
17

REFLECTION. The Patriarch Joseph was cast into a cistern and then taken out of it to be sold as a slave. God used the event to save the very brothers that had done him harm.

In response to Jesus' patience and prayers, God raised Him from His tomb so as to become the source of eternal salvation for all who desire to be His brothers and sisters.

PRAYER. *Almighty God, when beset by problems, help me to pray to You and to wait patiently for Your response.*

WILL exalt you, O Lord, for you have raised me out of the depths and have not let my enemies exult over me. —Ps 30:1

REFLECTION. On Good Friday, Jesus' enemies seemed to have been completely victorious over Him. But Easter Sunday proved them to be quite wrong.

We should be careful of seeming or temporary victories over those who have hurt us. If we do damage to our eternal souls, the victory will belong to our enemies, not us.

PRAYER. *Lord God, make me like Jesus Who did not strike back at His enemies but waited for Your help.*

 F THE Lord had not come to my aid, I would long ago have been consigned to the kingdom of silence. . . . your kindness, O Lord, raised me up. —Ps 94:17, 18b

REFLECTION. Life is noisy. Even when we are sound asleep; our breath can be heard. But with death, all sound ceases.

When Jesus died, God the Father did not let Him remain in the realm of silence; rather, He raised Him, so that both Jesus and His disciples might make a joyful noise unto the Lord.

PRAYER. *O God, let me hear in every sound the pulsation of the life that You bestow on Your creatures.*

E ASKED you for life, and you gave it to him, length of days forever and ever.
—Ps 21:5

APR. 20

REFLECTION. By the mere fact that we are alive, we assume that life is our possession. This is presumption, for we neither gave ourselves life nor can we keep ourselves alive indefinitely.

God's Son knew that His life came from the Father; thus, He asked Him for life and received it.

PRAYER. *Father, even as I may diet and exercise to achieve longevity, I look to You for the gift of eternal life.*

———

ING to the Lord a new song, for he has accomplished marvelous deeds. His right hand and his holy arm have made him victorious.
—Ps 98:1

APR. 21

REFLECTION. The Lord's deeds have always been awe-inspiring, as when He liberated the Israelites from Egypt, settled them in the Promised Land, and brought them back from exile.

But surpassing them all was Jesus' resurrection from the dead. This marvelous deed calls for an utterly new song.

PRAYER. *Lord, renew me completely, and put a new song of praise on my lips.*

WILL rejoice and exult in your kindness because you have witnessed my affliction and have taken note of my anguish. You have not abandoned me into the power of the enemy. **APR. 22** —Ps 31:8-9a

REFLECTION. Jesus had many enemies among His contemporaries. His worst "enemy" was Satan who had tempted Him to disobedience to God as a way to destroy Him.

Satan did not succeed, for Jesus carried out the Father's will to the end and God raised Him from the dead to a place at His right hand.

PRAYER. *O God, fill me with faith and defend me against the attacks of my ultimate enemy.*

 OU have granted him the desire of his heart and not withheld from him the request of his lips. **APR. 23** —Ps 21:3

REFLECTION. Jesus prayed for Himself and His disciples. From the Cross, He also prayed for those that made Him suffer: "Father, forgive them. . . ."

God answered Jesus' prayers by giving His tormentors the opportunity to repent. The first to do so was the centurion who supervised Jesus' execution; he acknowledged Jesus as God's Son.

PRAYER. *Holy Spirit, put on my lips prayers pleasing to the Father.*

HEN the Lord brought home the captives to Zion, we seemed to be dreaming. —Ps 126:1b

REFLECTION. When the exile in Babylon ended and many of the Jews returned home, they could hardly believe what was happening. It seemed like a dream.

Although Jesus had said He would rise, the disciples could not believe the women's news of the resurrection. They discounted it as the work of an overactive imagination.

PRAYER. *Almighty God, since to You everything is possible, may I never set limits to what You can accomplish in my life.*

LESSED are the people who know how to acclaim you, O Lord, who walk in the light of your countenance. —Ps 89:16

REFLECTION. The blind Bartimaeus pleaded with Jesus for the gift of sight. Receiving it, Jesus' face was the first thing he saw. The seeing Bartimaeus joined Jesus on the journey to His death and resurrection.

To the seeing, Jesus is light so that they might not stumble but walk securely in the path of dying and rising.

PRAYER. *O God, may we who follow Jesus, the true light, acclaim You now and through eternity.*

YOU have exalted above all things your name and your word. On the day I cried out, you answered me.

APR. 26

—Ps 138:2b-3a

REFLECTION. When Jesus cried out to the Father from the Cross, God answered Him by raising Him from the dead. In this, God is exalted as "Father," and so is His Son, Who is God's Word.

Because we believe in Jesus' resurrection, we too can and should cry out to God in our need and suffering—and at the hour of death.

PRAYER. *Loving Father, answer me when I cry out to You in sincerity of heart, just as You answered Jesus.*

 THIS is the day that the Lord has made; let us exult and rejoice in it.

APR. 27

—Ps 118:24

REFLECTION. While the Lord sustains the world every day by His power, He alone could and did bring life out of death on Easter. No one else could be credited with this.

Revealing the greatness of God's power and love, and filling us with a hope that transcends the grave, Easter is the feast of incomparable joy.

PRAYER. *O Lord, may the joy You give us at Easter overflow into every day of the year.*

YOU have turned my mourning into dancing; you have taken away my sackcloth and clothed me with joy. . . . O Lord, my God, I will praise you forever. —Ps 30:12, 13b

APR. 28

REFLECTION. Before His death, Jesus promised that His disciples would see Him again and then rejoice. Like a mother's labor pains that give way to joy when she holds her newborn child, the disciples' grief was turned to joy on Easter.

Because God has removed the source of our ultimate grief by Jesus' resurrection, we should be clothed with joy and overflowing with praise.

PRAYER. *O Lord, help me to express my joy outwardly that I may lift the spirits of those who are sad.*

_____

BUT he had sent a man ahead of them, Joseph, who had been sold as a slave. They shackled his feet with fetters . . . until what he had prophesied was fulfilled. . . . —Ps 105:17-19a

APR. 29

REFLECTION. The Patriarch Joseph was enslaved in Egypt and then liberated. By his life's course, he anticipated the domination and liberation of Israel.

Jesus suffered, died, and was buried, but then God liberated Him from the bonds of death—just as Jesus had prophesied. Jesus foreshadows the life of all who because of their relationship to Him call God their Father.

PRAYER. *Jesus, my Brother, make me a true child of God and an heir of eternal life.*

THE Lord looked down from his sanctuary on high and gazed on the earth from heaven, to hear the sighs of the prisoners and to set free those under sentence of death. —Ps 102:20-21

APR.

30

REFLECTION. Succumbing to temptation and sin, we are prisoners of the Evil One. The just sentence for our sins which damage our relationship to God is death—the death of our souls.

At the start of His mission, Jesus declared that God had anointed Him to set captives free. He died and rose that He might break the Evil One's stranglehold on humankind.

PRAYER. *O Lord, listen to my sighs and free me from sin and death.*

MANIFEST your works to your servants and your glory to their children. —Ps 90:16

MAY

1

REFLECTION. Created in God's image, we work as God Himself worked to make all things. Necessary though it be, our work is but a pale reflection of God's glorious work.

O that we could see more clearly God's work in the present! And how marvelous if God would soon manifest His glorious works to us by remaking all creation: new heavens and a new earth.

PRAYER. *O Lord, may our daily work be in harmony with Yours and prepare the way for the new creation.*

RISE up, O God, and defend your cause; remember how fools mock you all day long. **MAY 2**

—Ps 74:22

REFLECTION. It is important to discern what God thinks about the issues of human life. As His partners in furthering what is good in the world, it is just as important to act in His name.

It seems, however, that God Himself is sometimes slow in defending His cause. Undoubtedly, this is because He is patient with people who remain the object of His love even when they err.

PRAYER. *O God, I praise You for opening my mind and heart to what is right. Give me charity and patience with those who lack this understanding.*

O LORD, our Lord, how glorious is your name in all the earth! **MAY 3**

—Ps 8:2a

REFLECTION. We crave recognition. But Jesus lived to spread God's fame. He said: "I have made your name known to them, and I will continue to make it known."

Jesus spread God's name, "Father," so that we might know that He loves us utterly and without strings attached.

PRAYER. *Father, grant me the grace to desire Your esteem before that of others.*

THE Lord has clothed and girded himself with strength. —Ps 93:1b

MAY 4

REFLECTION. God clothed Himself with strength when saving Israel from its enemies and when rescuing Jesus from the jaws of death.

At our Baptism, we put on a white garment to show that God clothes us with Christ. If Christ remains our garment, He will one day clothe our corruptible nature with incorruptibility.

PRAYER. *O God, let me not worry about what I wear, but may You clothe me with compassion, kindness, humility, gentleness, and patience.*

THE Lord has indeed done great deeds for us, and we are overflowing with joy. —Ps 126:3

MAY 5

REFLECTION. St. Paul taught that Jesus died because of our sins and that He was raised so that we might be set right with God. In other words, the Son of God did not die and rise for His sake, but for our benefit.

We rejoice in this salvation and in the great love of God for us that motivated His great deeds.

PRAYER. *O Jesus, let no difficulties rob me of the joy that comes from the Easter mystery.*

BLESS our God, all you peoples; let the sound of his praise be heard. For he has preserved our lives. —Ps 66:8-9a

REFLECTION. God did not make death. Death entered the world through the devil's envy and human sin.

God desires to preserve and enhance human life. Thus He saved the Israelites again and again. Through Jesus, the Father has acted to save and elevate human life so that we can have abundance of life now and through eternity.

PRAYER. *Almighty God, I bless You for acting to preserve our lives through Jesus.*

WE HAVE escaped like a bird from the snare of the fowlers; the snare was broken, and we escaped. —Ps 124:7

REFLECTION. Perhaps we have had a "close call" with death or we know someone who has. We can only marvel and be thankful for such narrow escapes.

The psalmist questioned whether anyone could ultimately escape death. But someone did: Jesus Christ. And He is but the first of all those who believe in God through Him.

PRAYER. *O God, I thank You for making possible my own great escape.*

THE sea fled at the sight; the Jordan turned back. The mountains skipped like rams, the hills like lambs of the flock. —Ps 114:3-4

MAY 8

REFLECTION. When God brought Israel out of Egypt and into the Promised Land, all creation seemed to cooperate in His liberating and saving project. Bodies of water and hills made way for God's people.

We disciples of Jesus are also God's people, and creation will give way to God's power when He will raise our mortal bodies and make them like Jesus' glorious body.

PRAYER. *Father, help me to honor my body in preparation for its glorious transformation.*

LORD, I am your servant. I am your servant, the child of your handmaid; you have loosed my bonds. —Ps 116:16

MAY 9

REFLECTION. Sin and death are stronger than fallen human beings. They are masters, and fallen people are their servants.

We, however, are the children of God's handmaid, the Church. And if we submit daily to Christ, we shall be God's own servants. This will bring us the experience of utter freedom to do the good things we long to do.

PRAYER. *O my Jesus, by Your grace help me to flee other masters and submit entirely to You.*

THEIR hearts were not right with him, nor were they faithful to his covenant. Even so, he was compassionate toward them; he forgave their guilt and did not destroy them. **MAY 10** —Ps 78:37-38

REFLECTION. When the Israelites rebelled against the Lord Who loved and saved them, He forgave their wrongdoing and did not destroy them.

Similarly, when they killed Jesus, Whom God had sent, He did not obliterate them. Rather, God called them to faith and repentance.

PRAYER. *O God, by Your compassion make me always faithful to the New Covenant.*

YOU guide me with your counsel, and afterward you will receive me into glory. **MAY 11** —Ps 73:24

REFLECTION. God has given us uncommon counsel in Jesus, for example, that we must give up our life if we would truly gain it. Such counsel is vital if we would be received into glory.

All of Jesus' teachings have our salvation as their purpose, and we should let ourselves be guided by Him as sheep are led by a shepherd.

PRAYER. *Lord Jesus, may the hope of glory keep me faithful in following You through times of adversity and suffering.*

GOD has ascended amid shouts of joy; **MAY**
the Lord, amid the sound of trumpets.
—Ps 47:6

12

REFLECTION. When Jesus ascended to heaven, He did not abandon us but took His rightful place at God's right hand in order to become our advocate and to pour forth the Spirit.

As Jesus was taken up in glory, we too shall be glorified. As no glory on earth can compare with this heavenly glory, we do not compromise ourselves to attain earthly glory.

PRAYER. *O Jesus, while I sometimes look for the help of "friends in high places," grant me Your powerful help always.*

IN THE heavens he has placed a tent for the **MAY**
sun, which comes forth like a bridegroom
from his wedding chamber, rejoicing like an
athlete who runs his course. —Ps 19:5b-6

13

REFLECTION. Unusual solar phenomena at Gibeon in the Holy Land and at Fatima in Portugal were seen as signs of divine intervention.

Christians have always understood in this psalm a reference to Jesus, since He is also the Church's groom. As important as the sun is to life, Jesus is absolutely essential.

PRAYER. *Father, let the daily setting and rising of the sun remind me of Your Son's death and resurrection.*

HO is like the Lord, our God, the one who is enthroned on high and who stoops down to look on the heavens and the earth?

—Ps 113:5-6

REFLECTION. Although God is exceedingly great, He cares for His creatures and stoops down to help them, as in Israel's case. Such humility is God's trademark.

God lowered Himself most completely in His Son Jesus Who served His disciples and invited them to do likewise.

PRAYER. *Lord God, grant me the ambition of distinguishing myself by humble service.*

AY the favor of the Lord, our God, rest upon us. And may the work of our hands prosper—indeed, may the work of our hands prosper.

—Ps 90:17

REFLECTION. We sustain ourselves by our work. But we also express ourselves by our work. No two people will do the same work in the same way.

While some people work primarily with their minds, others work with their hands. In either case, although we put forth our best effort, it is God Who makes our work successful.

PRAYER. *Almighty God, I thank You for all my accomplishments and I pray that they might give You glory.*

HE Lord says to my Lord: "Sit at my right hand until I have made your enemies a footstool for you." The Lord will stretch forth from Zion your scepter of power. —Ps 110:1-2

MAY 16

REFLECTION. God promised that the Messiah would sit at His right hand in order to share His own throne and kingdom. This happened when Jesus ascended to heaven.

The Apostles brought this good news from Jerusalem to the ends of the earth, so that the power of Jesus' love might win over even His enemies to faith and love.

PRAYER. *Lord Jesus, to all my acquaintances make me Your emissary by charitable words and deeds.*

OU have exalted your majesty above the heavens. —Ps 8:2b

MAY 17

REFLECTION. From the moment that God created the earth and the heavens, God's majesty has been exalted by the heavens; their beauty tells God's glory.

But when God placed His Son at His right hand, God Himself exalted His majesty above the heavens. The Angels have ever since been praising Jesus, the Messiah, above the heavens.

PRAYER. *Father, by Your grace may I come one day to worship around the throne that You share with Jesus.*

YOU have given him dominion over the works of your hands and placed everything under his feet. —Ps 8:7

MAY 18

REFLECTION. Although God has given men and women dominion over His creation as its stewards, God has placed everything under Jesus' feet as the redeemer of all creation.

From His throne, Jesus is gently subjecting all men and women to Himself in order to remove us effectively from the power of Satan and prepare us for God's eternal kingdom.

PRAYER. *O God, in mind and heart, in thoughts and deeds, let me serve Jesus alone.*

 YOUR kingdom will last forever, and your dominion will endure throughout all generations. —Ps 145:13

MAY 19

REFLECTION. What kingdom ruled by mortal kings has endured through all generations? None. What earthly kingdom can hope to last forever? None.

But Jesus' kingdom, which He shares with the Father, will last forever and all Who enter Jesus' realm will also inherit everlasting life.

PRAYER. *Father, by Your grace may I enter now and remain forever with Your Son in the everlasting kingdom.*

HE scepter of your kingdom will be a scepter of justice. —Ps 45:7b

REFLECTION. Kings and other leaders often use their position and power to ensure that their own interests are served, not necessarily that the right thing is done for the people.

Seated on God's throne, Jesus is not this kind of king. He uses His scepter or power to secure what is right and just for each of us. Jesus will never short-change us!

PRAYER. *Lord Jesus, help me to be just with everyone—and, indeed, to treat them much better than they might deserve.*

 F I ascend to the heavens, you are there. —Ps 139:8a

REFLECTION. Ascending to the heavens is not like climbing a mountain, a feat that requires skill and great effort. Ascending to the heavens requires faith in God and in Jesus Who Himself ascended there by fidelity to His Father.

When God takes us there by His power, we shall be united with Jesus Who has preceded us to be our hope and inspiration.

PRAYER. *Almighty God, grant us to bow down with Jesus in humble service to others so as to be exalted in due time by Your mighty hand.*

HEN you send forth your Spirit, they are created, and you renew the face of the earth. —Ps 104:30

MAY 22

REFLECTION. God promised to seal the new covenant by granting to men and women a new spirit, His Spirit. This first happened at Pentecost and to each of us at Baptism.

Since God makes no distinctions but gives His Spirit to all who are open to receiving Him, the Spirit creates unity among humankind. How the face of the earth could be changed by such openness!

PRAYER. *God, send forth Your Spirit again to renew my own face in warm welcome and mercy towards others.*

 O NOT cast me out from your presence or take away from me your Holy Spirit. —Ps 51:13

MAY 23

REFLECTION. When God breathed His Spirit into the first man, he became a living being. God's Spirit became the source of the life—the matchless life—of men and women.

If God were to take His Spirit from us, or if we ourselves were to drive the Spirit out, we would sink into inhumanity and extinction.

PRAYER. *Almighty God, keep Your Spirit in me and in all who are tempted to push the Spirit out of their lives.*

YOU give them to drink from your delightful streams. For with you is the fountain of life. —Ps 36:9b-10a **MAY 24**

Jesus invited the thirsty to drink the living waters that would flow from Him. He was speaking of the Holy Spirit that He would pour forth when He was glorified.

When we are parched, we hydrate ourselves to regain our energy. When we are lifeless in our pursuit of the Christian life—unable to love or to forgive—we can be filled with the waters of the Spirit by prayer and the Sacraments.

PRAYER. *Lord Jesus, irrigate me daily with the waters of Your Spirit.*

AT THE waters of Meribah they angered the Lord. . . . For they rebelled against the Spirit of God. —Ps 106:32a, 33a **MAY 25**

REFLECTION. Although God gave Israel water in the desert, they doubted Him and rebelled against Him. They would not obey.

Jesus and St. Peter would later teach that God gives the Spirit to those who obey Him. The Spirit comes to the aid of those who are willing to do as God directs, yet find it difficult.

PRAYER. *Lord, grant me the grace of obedience and the humility to seek Your Spirit's assistance.*

HERE can I go to hide from your spirit? Where can I flee from your presence? —Ps 139:7

MAY 26

REFLECTION. The Holy Spirit scrutinizes everything, even the depths of God. Thus, the Spirit knows each of us much better than we know ourselves, and He can disclose us to ourselves.

Indeed, God knows the intentions of human hearts, so that the Spirit Himself prays in us and intercedes for us more perfectly than our feeble words can express.

PRAYER. *Spirit of God, teach me what I should know about myself and move me to pray as I ought.*

 N THE day I cried out, you answered me and granted strength to my spirit. —Ps 138:3

MAY 27

REFLECTION. While human flesh is often weak, our spirit too is sometimes weak. The Holy Spirit can communicate to our spirit His strength.

In fact, Jesus told His timid Apostles that He would clothe them with power from on high—that is, the Holy Spirit. The Book of Acts shows just how powerful the Apostles became.

PRAYER. *O God, I am often lacking in strength; grant me power from on high.*

O MATTER how faint my spirit is within me, you are there to guide my steps.
—Ps 142:4

MAY 28

REFLECTION. God's Spirit bears witness to our spirit that we are God's children and heirs, so that if we suffer with Jesus then we shall also rule with Him.

The Holy Spirit does not lead us into subjection and fear, but into love and boldness when we call out to Him, "Abba, Father."

PRAYER. *Father, in my confusion and weakness, do not fail to guide me as You guided Jesus' Apostles to spread the Good News.*

 Y WHOLE being will say, "O Lord, who is there like you? . . ."
—Ps 35:10a

MAY 29

REFLECTION. The Lord God is utterly unique. Moses and David and Solomon affirmed this, and God Himself insisted on it through Isaiah. The New Testament shows us the ultimate reason: the one and only God is a community of three equally divine Persons.

At the same time, God has created human beings uniquely in His image and likeness, so that we bear the imprint of the Trinity in our instinct for community and closeness to others.

PRAYER. *O Lord, help me not to withdraw into myself but to reach out continually to others.*

THE heavens were made by the word of the Lord, and all their host by the breath of his mouth. —Ps 33:6

MAY 30

REFLECTION. The Lord God or Father made everything. Yet He was assisted by His Word and His Breath, that is, His Spirit. The Persons of the Trinity acted together in creation, and they still act in communion with one another.

In the Church and beyond her boundaries, we are called to unity and collaboration. It takes teamwork to make the world go round.

PRAYER. *O Blessed Trinity, teach and move humankind to cooperate for the world's well-being.*

I WILL make haste and not delay to observe your precepts. —Ps 119:60

MAY 31

REFLECTION. When the Virgin Mary learned that her cousin Elizabeth was with child, she quickly went to help her. Mary did not dwell on her own pregnancy; rather, without even being asked, she responded to Elizabeth's need.

By the parable of the Good Samaritan, Jesus taught that keeping God's commandment to love our neighbor means we must be willing to help those in need, even when inconvenient.

PRAYER. *O Jesus, give me a heart of love for those who are in need.*

ET those who love the Lord hate evil, for he protects the souls of his faithful ones and rescues them from the hand of the wicked. **JUNE 1** —Ps 97:10

REFLECTION. Like the fruit that looked good in the Garden of Eden, evil often seems good. So even if we love God, it is easy for us to be drawn to evil.

We must get beyond the appearance of goodness and make a decisive break with evil, for evil is corrosive and destructive of those who entertain it.

PRAYER. *Almighty God, protect me and rescue me from evil. Help me to love You and be attached to You alone.*

 END forth your light and your truth; they will serve as my guide. Let them bring me to your holy mountain, to the place of your dwelling. **JUNE 2** —Ps 43:3

REFLECTION. God sent forth His light in Jesus, Who is the Light of the World. And through Jesus' teaching He sent His truth in the Holy Spirit to the Apostles.

Thus, God brought humankind to the place of His dwelling, that is, the Church. In the Church, we experience God's presence, and there we receive guidance for our life's pilgrimage.

PRAYER. *Father, I thank You for moving out of Yourself through Your Son and Spirit to draw me into Your Trinitarian life.*

E FILLED them with bread from heaven. **JUNE**
—Ps 105:40b

3

REFLECTION. The Lord filled the children of Israel with manna, bread from heaven, as He led them to the Promised Land. Yet, as Jesus observed, this gift did not keep them from dying.

Jesus fed the crowds in deserted places, but He stressed that He Himself was the true bread from heaven. "Whoever eats this bread will live forever."

PRAYER. *O God, even while I worry about eating nutritiously, help me never to neglect the necessary nourishment You provide: Jesus in the Holy Eucharist.*

RAISE the Lord, O Jerusalem! Glorify **JUNE** your God, O Zion! . . . He brings peace to your borders and fills you with the finest wheat. —Ps 147:12, 14

4

REFLECTION. For centuries God provided healthful nourishment for His holy city, Jerusalem, and kept its inhabitants together in safety.

God superseded His generosity to Israel in the Church that is nourished by the sacramental bread of Jesus' Body. By means of the Eucharist, the Church is fortified in unity and peace as Christ's Mystical Body in the world.

PRAYER. *Help me, O God, to recognize and honor Christ's Mystical Body, the Church, every time I partake of His Eucharistic Body.*

E HAS granted deliverance to his people and established his covenant forever; holy and awe-inspiring is his name. —Ps 111:9

REFLECTION. God granted Israel deliverance from slavery and exile. Through Jesus, He granted all people deliverance from sin and death, for Jesus forged a new covenant with humankind by writing God's law on our hearts and giving us the Spirit.

God's name is recognized as holy by Jesus' disciples because of the deliverance He has accomplished.

PRAYER. *Father, may Your name be hallowed or acknowledged as holy by all people.*

 S YOUR kindness celebrated in the grave, or your faithfulness in the tomb? Are your wonders known in the region of darkness, or your righteous deeds in the land of oblivion? —Ps 88:12-13

REFLECTION. The questions posed by the psalmist were answered by God through Christ. Between His death and resurrection, Christ descended into the region of the dead to make known God's wonders and to take out of it the righteous dead.

When we are feeling dead, Jesus can certainly deliver us from our gloom by His good news.

PRAYER. *Jesus, help me to tune in to Your good news daily, especially when I feel hopeless.*

AY you be blessed by the Lord, the **JUNE 7** Maker of heaven and earth. The heavens belong to the Lord, but he has given the earth to humanity.

—Ps 115:15-16

REFLECTION. Since God created all things, everything belongs ultimately to Him. But the heavens are properly His sphere, as human beings cannot ascend there.

By becoming a man, the Son of God gained a foothold on earth; and by rising from the dead and ascending to the Father, He gained for humanity a place in heaven.

PRAYER. *O God, as I keep my sights on heaven, may Your grace move me to make the earth a better place.*

———————

 RUST in him at all times, my people, **JUNE 8** and pour out your heart before him.

—Ps 62:9

REFLECTION. In Jesus, God has earned our total trust; for to reconcile us to God, Jesus gave His all on Calvary. Pierced by a soldier's lance, blood and water flood from His heart.

We pour out our hearts in prayer to God because it is not possible that He Who did not spare His own Son for our sakes will not give us all things with Him.

PRAYER. *Sacred Heart of Jesus, because I trust in You, I cast all my concerns on You Who care for me.*

ITH the Lord there is kindness, as well as plenteous redemption. He alone will redeem Israel from all its sins. **JUNE 9** —Ps 130:7b-8

REFLECTION. In the ancient world, many people became slaves because they could not pay their debts. But a relative or friend could pay for them; in this case, the slave was redeemed and freed.

Jesus taught that to commit sin is to be its slave. Only God could and did redeem us from sin, which can be so powerful a master. He did it through Christ.

PRAYER. *Almighty God, through the grace of Your Son keep me free from sin today.*

OD is truly good to the upright, to those who are pure in heart. **JUNE 10** —Ps 73:1

REFLECTION. If all that makes us impure proceeds from within, then our hearts must be pure to be upright in our words and deeds.

The Blessed Virgin Mary heard the word of God and kept it, just as she also treasured the memory of all God's actions in her life. Her heart was immaculate.

PRAYER. *O God, I desire Mary's immaculate heart. Purify my heart with the word of Jesus.*

E HAS remembered his kindness and his fidelity to the house of Israel. The farthest ends of the earth have witnessed the salvation of our God.

—Ps 98:3

REFLECTION. Our God is the God of Israel. As the Lord redeemed Israel, He sent His salvation forth also to the ends of the earth. As Jesus said, "Salvation is from the Jews."

God has not jettisoned His original people by including believers from all nations. God remains faithful, and His kindness is for all. Can the same be said of us?

PRAYER. O Lord, while Your salvation has happily reached the ends of earth, let me see it closer to home in my own conversion.

EMEMBER the people that you purchased long ago, the tribe that you redeemed as your own possession.

—Ps 74:2a

REFLECTION. We generally give something to get something. Some acquisitions are cheap; others are costly. God paid highly to acquire Israel who were often an embarrassment to Him.

To acquire a new people encompassing every nation, God paid with the blood of His Son. Though humankind was an expensive purchase, in His love God deemed us worth it.

PRAYER. O Jesus, when discipleship becomes costly, help me to respond generously.

HE mouth of the righteous man utters wisdom, and his tongue speaks what is right. —Ps 37:30

JUNE 13

REFLECTION. The Apostle James said, "From the same mouth come blessing and cursing." Under the spell of sin, mouths are like open graves and tongues drip with venom. Under the influence of grace, mouths utter only what is good and edifying.

Ultimately, saintly mouths speak only of Christ and Him crucified.

PRAYER. *Holy God, purify my lips that I may only and always proclaim Your praise.*

 HE Lord has founded a city on the holy mountains. He loves the gates of Zion more than any dwelling in Jacob. Glorious things are said of you, O city of God. —Ps 87:1-3

JUNE 14

REFLECTION. Jerusalem was the city of God's dwelling, where He was worshiped rightly. Glorious to behold, its time and its importance faded because of human sin.

Through Jesus, God founded a spiritual city upon the foundation stones of the twelve Apostles. Glorious things are said of the Church since she is the mother of innumerable saints shining with the glory of Christ Himself.

PRAYER. *Lord God, may Your love for the Church renew her in our time for the praise and glory of Your name.*

ELIVER me, O Lord, from lying lips and from deceitful tongues.
—Ps 120:2

REFLECTION. Little else is as destructive as the sinful human tongue. Jesus suffered because of tongues that opposed Him, betrayed Him, denied Him, lied about Him, and condemned Him.

Jesus used His tongue to speak the truth and to offer forgiveness. And when He called out to the Father for deliverance from His enemies, His prayer was heard.

PRAYER. *Almighty God, grant me the grace to control my tongue and to use it to help and edify others.*

ONCERNING them it can be said, "This one was born there." However, of Zion it will be said, "They were all born there," for the Most High himself establishes her."
—Ps 87:4b-5

REFLECTION. Most cities keep birth records. We may identify with and take pride in the city of our birth.

But all Christians everywhere were born spiritually in God's city, the Jerusalem above, our mother; for it was from the Church's teaching that we received the faith, and we are nursed at her breast by the Sacraments.

PRAYER. *Father, I thank You for the Church that is the mother of all Your children.*

RAISE the Lord from the heavens; offer praise to him in the heights! Praise him, all his angels; offer praise to him, all his hosts! . . . Praise the Lord from the earth, you sea monsters and ocean depths.

JUNE 17

—Ps 148:1-2, 7

REFLECTION. As God once made the heavens and the earth, and now makes everything new through the risen Christ, all creatures in both spheres are summoned to give Him praise.

One day all creation will be set free from its bondage and share the glorious freedom of God's children. We who have already received this freedom should anticipate the song of all creation.

PRAYER. *O Lord, let my mouth never be lacking in praise for You.*

OW wonderful and delightful it is for brothers to live together in unity.

JUNE 18

—Ps 133:1

REFLECTION. The risen Jesus referred to His disciples as His brothers. And He poured into them the Holy Spirit so that they might be one with each other and with Him in His Body, the Church.

When the members of the Church live in unity, they taste the unity of the Persons of the Trinity and they help the world to believe that God is love.

PRAYER. *O God, help me to accept, appreciate, and love my fellow Christians.*

AND as they play, they all sing, "In you are all my fountains." —Ps 87:7

JUNE 19

REFLECTION. The psalmist rejoiced in Jerusalem because its fountains could quench his thirst. In the heavenly Jerusalem, life-giving water will come from the throne of God and the Lamb.

But Jesus assured the Samaritan woman at the well that she could receive this living water from Him without waiting. We receive it through the Church's Sacraments.

PRAYER. *Lord Jesus, when I am weary, refresh me with the grace of the Holy Spirit.*

WHAT we had heard, we have now beheld for ourselves in the city of the Lord of hosts, in the city of our God that he established to endure forever. —Ps 48:9

JUNE 20

REFLECTION. Tourists to the world's great cities know them at first by hearsay and then by personal experience. We know the heavenly Jerusalem from what John the seer of Revelation told us.

Since John was a prophet, his words are a divine testimony. Yet even they remain less than adequate as a description of what God has prepared for those who love Him.

PRAYER. *Almighty God, we have here no lasting city. Fill me with a desire for the heavenly Jerusalem.*

HERE the thrones of judgment were established, the thrones of the house of David. —Ps 122:5

REFLECTION. During the Last Supper, Jesus promised the Apostles that they would sit on thrones to judge the twelve tribes of Israel. As themselves recipients of God's mercy, the Apostles will surely judge mercifully.

No one, indeed, needs to fear future judgment if he has been merciful with his neighbors.

PRAYER. *O Lord, if the measure with which I measure others will be used to measure me, then make me merciful towards everyone.*

UT I am like a green olive tree in the house of God. I place my trust forever and ever in the kindness of God. —Ps 52:10

REFLECTION. Those who care little for God are on the way to ruin, but those who are faithful to Him flourish like the olive tree. This is because they place their trust not in themselves but in God's kindness.

They grow in the orchard of God's house, which is the Church or the Body of Christ, from Whom they draw their fruitfulness as branches on a vine.

PRAYER. *Father, keep me rooted firmly in the Church in order that I may bear good fruit.*

YOU created my inmost being; you knit me together in my mother's womb.

—Ps 139:13

JUNE 23

REFLECTION. From the womb, God consecrates each of us to Himself, as He did Jeremiah, John the Baptist, and Paul.

For what role in His plan has God called and consecrated me? Am I grateful for the unique configuration of talents and inadequacies, strengths and weaknesses that are mine?

PRAYER. *O God, Elizabeth and Zachary, called their baby "John," which means "the Lord is gracious." Help me to recognize Your goodness in making me who I am.*

 YOU shook the earth and split it apart; repair its cracks, for it continues to shake. You have inflicted hardships on your people; you have given us wine that made us stagger.

—Ps 60:4-5

JUNE 24

REFLECTION. Earthquakes are uniquely unsettling, disturbing, frightening. Yet they can represent all earth-shattering events that happen in our individual lives.

These events may cause us to be disoriented and stagger for a time. But when we recall that God holds power over them, we know Whom to approach to gain relief.

PRAYER. *Lord God, we cannot control many events. Help us to call upon You Who can.*

E WHO guards you will not fall asleep. Indeed, the one who guards Israel never slumbers, never sleeps. **JUNE 25**

—Ps 121:3b-4

REFLECTION. Because God loves His people, He watches over them as parents protect their children. Parents don't always succeed in this regard because of overwork or tiredness.

God never fails to guard His people. When bad things happen, it may be that we have fled God's protection or that He has allowed harm to come to us for a greater good to be realized only later.

PRAYER. *O Lord, let me never flee from Your protection nor doubt Your love when bad things happen to me.*

OU rulers, do you render justice? Do you judge your people impartially? No! You devise wickedness in your hearts, and your hands bring about violence on the earth. **JUNE 26**

—Ps 58:2-3

REFLECTION. The truth cannot be denied. And the truth is that human leaders often play favorites and frequently care little for fairness; rather, they care for themselves and their interests.

Knowing this, we do not reject human leaders. We do, however, refuse to put our stock in them. We put our stock in God, and we pray to Him on their behalf.

PRAYER. *Almighty God, You know the hearts of all. Change the hearts of leaders to be just and to pursue fairness.*

S THE mountains surround Jerusalem, so the Lord surrounds his people both now and forevermore. —Ps 125:2

JUNE 27

REFLECTION. Like the mountains, the Lord protects Jerusalem. Not His power or strength, but God Himself surrounds His people, and He does so always.

As the mountains did not completely preserve Jerusalem from harm, so also God's encompassing presence is not a guarantee against all damage, but a pledge of accompaniment at all times.

PRAYER. *O God, no matter what happens to me, be with me and sustain my faith and courage.*

 OU let our captors ride over our heads, and we went through fire and water, but now you have afforded us relief. —Ps 66:12

JUNE 28

REFLECTION. As parents let children alone to their mischief so that they might learn from its consequences, so God leaves us to sin. But God does not like it one bit. Our loving and forgiving Father relieves the suffering we cause ourselves and others.

Indeed, God wants us to refrain from evil and to relieve others' suffering. We should hasten to do both.

PRAYER. *Father, sometimes You let us fall and get hurt. Pick us up quickly and move us to run to the aid of others.*

THE angel of the Lord encamps around those who fear God, and he delivers them. —Ps 34:8

JUNE 29

REFLECTION. As in the Exodus God's Angel protected and rescued Israel, so also His Angel protected and delivered Saints Peter and Paul in order that they might establish God's new people.

God guards and saves His people. Therefore, we should not fear others. Our fear—in the sense of reverence or awe—should be reserved for God and stimulate us to serve and obey Him.

PRAYER. *Jesus, may Your perfect love cast out all my misplaced fear, while motivating me to work out my salvation "in fear and trembling."*

COME forth! Let us bow down to worship him; let us kneel before the Lord, our Maker. For he is our God, and we are the people he shepherds, the flock he protects. —Ps 95:6-7a

JUNE 30

REFLECTION. There is no such thing as a "self-made man." God is our Maker and we are His creatures. We acknowledge this bodily by kneeling down to Him in adoration.

We do this readily because God loves us. He shepherds us so that we may not become irremediably lost, and He protects us so that we may not get irreparably hurt.

PRAYER. *O Lord, help me to adore You, especially in the Blessed Sacrament.*

YOU fixed all the boundaries of the earth and created both summer and winter. **JULY 1**
—Ps 74:17

REFLECTION. Most of us prefer predictability and uniformity. God prefers surprise and variety. He created an assortment of landscapes, climates, and seasons.

The cold and dark of winter destroy bacteria and make us serious and reflective. The summer sun warms our bodies and lifts our spirits. Each season brings its own benefits and gifts.

PRAYER. *Almighty God, grant me the grace to make the most of each season and to profit from all Your gifts.*

HOW precious to me are your designs, O God! How vast in number they are! If I were to attempt to count them, they would outnumber the grains of sand. **JULY 2**
—Ps 139:17-18a

REFLECTION. Artists specialize in designs. God is the greatest artist of all. This is evident in nature, but also in the designs that He has for His creatures.

He has a unique plan for each one of us. Given the number of creatures, God's designs are innumerable.

PRAYER. *Lord God, let the countless grains of sand remind me of the vastness of Your designs and help me to appreciate Your unique plan for me.*

WAKEN and be diligent in my defense; come to my aid, my God and my Lord. —Ps 35:23

JULY 3

REFLECTION. Because the risen Jesus missed Thomas the first time, He returned the following Sunday to appear to him as well. Thomas then believed that Jesus was Lord and God.

Indeed, Thomas affirmed that Jesus was "*my* Lord and *my* God" because Jesus had given him special consideration and cared about him personally.

PRAYER. *O God, grant me the grace to declare with St. Paul, "I live by faith in the Son of God who has loved me and given himself up for me."*

LESSED is the nation whose God is the Lord. —Ps 33:12a

JULY 4

REFLECTION. Israel discovered long ago that they were privileged to have the Lord as their God, for He blessed them abundantly. But the Lord did not limit this privilege to them.

All people who obey God can experience His blessings. The forefathers and founders of America believed this. Despite its failures, America has been abundantly blessed.

PRAYER. *O Lord, help all believers to share their faith and Your wisdom with their fellow citizens so that future generations may prosper.*

WILL walk in complete freedom because I have sought your commands. —Ps 119:45

JULY
5

REFLECTION. Freedom is not the license to do evil. Rather, it is the self-control to do what is right and good—which, in our heart of hearts, we desire to do.

God's commands, being in harmony with the truest part of ourselves, help us to achieve self-control and true freedom. "Where the Spirit of the Lord is, there is freedom. . . ."

PRAYER. *Lord, stir up the Spirit of the New Covenant in me so that I may keep Your law.*

 Y HEART is steadfast, O God, my heart is steadfast. —Ps 57:8

JULY
6

REFLECTION. Trees sway in the wind. They cannot decide to withstand it as they have no will. But we do have a will, and yet we waver. We compromise. We do not remain faithful to God.

Human infidelity starts in the heart. By staying close to Jesus we receive from Him the steadfastness that brought Him to the Cross and beyond.

PRAYER. *Almighty God, I thank you for Jesus and for the martyrs who inspire me to remain steadfast and faithful to You.*

LORD, you are my allotted portion and my cup. . . . I have truly received a wonderful inheritance.

—Ps 16:5a, 6b

REFLECTION. Each of us can only have so much and no more. But what we have includes nothing less—no one less—than the Lord Himself.

The Lord is especially the portion of those to whom He has given a religious vocation. They forego many benefits in this world in order to focus on God and His service.

PRAYER. *O God, may You call many more men and women to religious life, and strengthen me in my own vocation.*

HE fool says in his heart, "There is no God." Such are depraved and their deeds are vile.

—Ps 53:2

REFLECTION. Those who deny God's existence sometimes fall into the trap of putting something else in God's place, such as power or money; and its attainment becomes of paramount significance.

Those who deny God also lose a sense of the common origin they share with others. Violence against others is, then, a short step away.

PRAYER. *Almighty God, bring to faith unbelievers so that the world may be spared the awful effects of foolishness.*

LIE down and sleep; I awaken again, for the
Lord sustains me.
—Ps 3:6

REFLECTION. Children dislike being put to bed because by sleeping they lose out on the action and excitement of life. We fear that it is like this with death, which is unending sleep.

But Jesus said that the dead, such as Lazarus and Jairus' daughter were only sleeping, and then he awakened them to life! He will do the same for us if we depend on Him to save us.

PRAYER. *O God, help me to live to the full by loving. Raise me then to eternal life in Your kingdom.*

LORD, who may dwell in your sanctuary? Who may abide on your holy
mountain? The one who leads a
blameless life and does what is right.
—Ps 15:1-2a

REFLECTION. Sometimes we are tempted to think that by making sacrifices we can have easier access to God. But God is not pleased by our sacrifices if they are a substitute for moral living.

Indeed, what pleases God most is our forgiveness of those who have failed morally, for both Hosea and Jesus spoke for God, saying, "I desire mercy and not sacrifice."

PRAYER. *O God, help me always to do what is right and to forgive those who don't—that is, to be like You.*

HOSE who seek the Lord want for no good thing. Come, my children, listen to me; I will teach you the fear of the Lord. —Ps 34:11b-12

JULY 11

REFLECTION. Jesus wants to give us an abundant life, and He taught us how to get it: "Seek first God's kingdom and his righteousness, and all these things will be given you besides."

Often the fear of missing out on good things drives us. Would we not do better making God and what pleases Him our first concern?

PRAYER. *O God, help me to live as St. Benedict taught: to prefer nothing whatever to Christ Himself.*

 GOD, do not remain silent; do not be quiet and inactive, O God. —Ps 83:2

JULY 12

REFLECTION. Given our prideful tendency to boast, wisdom would dictate that we should prefer silence to talking. But since God does not share our sinful tendencies, no such precautions are warranted on His part.

Injustice cries out from the earth and summons God to intervene as the Only One Who can effectively counteract evil.

PRAYER. *O Lord, let me never be silent when I should open my mouth to call upon You.*

N RETURN for my love they denounce me even as I offer up prayers for them. They give me back evil in exchange for good and hatred in place of my love. —Ps 109:4-5

REFLECTION. This captures Jesus' experience: in return for His love, He received hatred. How can His disciples expect something different for themselves if they truly follow Him?

Despite mistreatment, we should pursue love because it is its own reward. We can, moreover, also expect the reward God gave Jesus: eternal life.

PRAYER. *Father, help me to love the unlovable—indeed, even those who hate me.*

 REJOICE in your word, like one who discovers a great treasure. —Ps 119:162

REFLECTION. People hold on tightly to what they treasure, whether they be objects or people.

If our hearts are wherever our treasure may be, then we do not want to treasure what can disappear or slip away from us. Jesus indicated that the whole universe as we know it will pass, but His word will remain.

PRAYER. *O God, I give thanks for Jesus and His word. Increase my appreciation of the value of Your word.*

OME forth to bless the Lord, all you servants of the Lord, who minister throughout the night in the house of the Lord. **JULY 15** —Ps 134:1

REFLECTION. The Lord's servants are invited to bless the Lord throughout the night. Christian monks have responded to this invitation by rising to pray during the night, as Jesus Himself did.

While a worthy practice, this psalm's ultimate invitation is for us to praise God even when the harsh and painful circumstances of our lives plunge us into darkness.

PRAYER. *O Lord, when night descends on my soul, grant me the grace to persevere in prayer.*

 HOSE who chase after other gods only multiply their sorrows. **JULY 16** —Ps 16:4a

REFLECTION. At Mount Sinai, God commanded that Israel should not serve other gods. At Mount Carmel, Elijah asked Israel to choose to serve either God or Baal. On a mount in Galilee, Jesus observed that no one could serve both God and mammon.

We often seek out money and success over God because we imagine that they will bring us security. We are mistaken.

PRAYER. *O Lord, while I profess with my lips that You alone are God, let this be reflected in my daily choices and actions.*

YOU deliver those who are weak from those who are too strong for them, and you protect the poor and needy from those who seek to exploit them.

—Ps 35:10b

REFLECTION. As the Virgin Mary proclaimed in her *Magnificat*, the Lord secures justice. He casts down the mighty from their thrones and lifts up the lowly.

To know this is critical, because it keeps us from justifying evil means to attain justice.

PRAYER. *O God, help me to dedicate myself to prayerful discernment as I collaborate with You in the promotion of justice.*

IF ONLY you would listen to his voice today.

—Ps 95:7b

REFLECTION. Voices are distinctive, and human beings have the capacity for recognizing hundreds of them. Thus, when we hear the voice of a friend we may be reassured. When it is the voice of an enemy, we might cringe.

The voice that is both attractive and difficult to listen to is that of Christ. He is the Good Shepherd Who goes ahead of His sheep and lays down His life for them. We can follow Him—if we but listen.

PRAYER. *Lord, filter out of my head all the voices that distract me and keep me from listening to You.*

ET everything that breathes offer praise to the Lord. Alleluia. —Ps 150:6

REFLECTION. Because God created us by the sharing of His breath, and since He renews us with the outpouring of His Spirit, we should become creation's voice, praising God.

Every breath we take recalls our creation by God and should serve to remind us to praise Him for our life—temporal and eternal.

PRAYER. *Almighty God, I praise You for calling me into life, and I beg You to move me to praise You continually.*

 HE stone that the builders rejected has become the cornerstone. This is the Lord's doing, and it is marvelous in our eyes. —Ps 118:22-23

REFLECTION. Jesus was rejected and killed, but He became the cornerstone of the Church that is the temple of the Holy Spirit.

We who are members of Jesus' temple may sometimes experience rejection for Jesus' sake. When we do so, we should count ourselves blessed!

PRAYER. *O God, both when we are doing well and when we are not, may we be convinced that You have not rejected us.*

PROCLAIM that the Lord is God. He made us and we are his possession; we are his people, the flock he shepherds.

JULY 21

—Ps 100:3

REFLECTION. God has made everyone, and all belong to Him. But those to whom He has shown Himself through Jesus belong to Him in a special way, for He has also redeemed them by the Blood of the Lamb.

All Christians are the sheep of Jesus' flock. Sadly, it has become divided. We should strive and pray so that there will be one flock, just as there is one Shepherd.

PRAYER. *Lord Jesus, inflame all Christian hearts with the desire for unity.*

 GOD, you are my God, for whom I have been searching earnestly. My soul yearns for you and my body thirsts for you, like the earth when it is parched.

JULY 22

—Ps 63:2

REFLECTION. Jesus asked His first would-be disciples, "What do you seek?" They were not quite sure. Jesus put a similar question to Mary Magdalene, "Whom do you seek?" To her positive response, Jesus manifested Himself as the risen Lord.

As worthwhile as the many things we seek may be, none can satisfy us as can Jesus.

PRAYER. *Father, help me to be in touch with my deepest needs and to perceive in Jesus the One Who can satisfy them.*

108

FOR your sake we are put to death all day long; we are treated like sheep destined to be slaughtered. —Ps 44:23 **JULY 23**

REFLECTION. In some parts of the world, Christians are abused or even killed for their faith. Christians who live elsewhere are generally not aware of such persecution.

Where Christianity is tolerated, it is often treated by the larger society as irrelevant. Such treatment does not kill bodies, but it weakens souls—and it does so silently.

PRAYER. *O Lord, encourage Your faithful who are persecuted, and strengthen in faith those who live where Christianity is treated with indifference.*

YOU led your people like a flock by the hand of Moses and Aaron. —Ps 77:21 **JULY 24**

REFLECTION. Israel became God's people, His flock. Yet they were led by Moses and Aaron whom God chose for this task. God's Son chose Peter and the other Apostles to tend God's new people and feed His sheep.

The flock is still led by those whom Jesus calls: the Pope, bishops, priests, deacons, and religious. They are critical to our well-being.

PRAYER. *O Lord, grant insight and wisdom and love to those who shepherd us in Your name.*

THOSE who go forth weeping, carrying the seeds to be sown, will return with shouts of joy, carrying their sheaves.

JULY 25

—Ps 126:6

REFLECTION. Farmers must part with some of their grain and sow it in order to reap the next harvest.

Observing that the seed must die to bear fruit, Jesus taught that whoever would gain life must lose it. This is most obvious in the martyrs whose death gained for them eternal life and acted as the seed of others' faith.

PRAYER. *O God, help me to give up my life like St. James did for the spread of God's word.*

THE kindness of the Lord is with those who fear him, and his righteousness with their children's children, with those who keep his covenant. —Ps 103:17-18a

JULY 26

REFLECTION. Parents transmit to their children more than their genes. They pass on their ideas, values, and behaviors. They also pass on their faith and obedience to God.

The young absorb consciously and unconsciously life's most important lessons from the adults they know. Such is our responsibility for future generations.

PRAYER. *O Lord, help me to live with greater reverence for You and with greater concern for the effect of my example on the young.*

THE Lord redeems the lives of those who serve him. —Ps 34:23a

JULY 27

REFLECTION. So many people require our service: our family members, our co-workers, our clients, and our neighbors. God does not need us to do things for Him, but He is served indirectly every time we take care of others' needs.

The only way this happens is if we come into His presence to praise Him and learn from Him. Being with the Lord is not the only thing we must do, but it comes before our serving others.

PRAYER. *Lord Jesus, help me to be like Martha and Mary, not just one or the other.*

MOSES and Aaron were among his priests, and Samuel was among those who invoked his name; they cried out to the Lord, and he answered them. —Ps 99:6

JULY 28

REFLECTION. Priests function as intermediaries or "go-betweens." On others' behalf they invoke God for His assistance and blessing.

God answered the prayers of Moses and Aaron and Samuel. He answered the prayers of Jesus, our great High Priest, and God will certainly answer the prayers of Jesus' priests of the New Covenant.

PRAYER. *Almighty God, may the prayers of our priests find a favorable hearing before You.*

111

I AM A friend to all who fear you, all who observe your commands. —Ps 119:63

REFLECTION. Friends initially come together because they find one another mutually intriguing, but friends remain together when they share common interests and goals.

Among our friends there should be people who have great reverence for the Lord and keep His commands. Their dedication will feed our own.

PRAYER. *Lord, fill my circle of friends with Your friends so that I may be a true disciple.*

HAVE mercy on me, O Lord, for I am tottering; help me, O Lord, for my body is in agony. My soul is also filled with anguish. But you, O Lord—how long? —Ps 6:3-4

REFLECTION. God's faithful people are not immune from physical and spiritual affliction. And they experience the same emotional turmoil that accompanies the suffering of non-believers.

But believers live their suffering in the presence of God, manifest their anguish to Him, and invoke His help with trust and hope.

PRAYER. *Almighty God, in my suffering move me to turn to You with faith and hope and trust.*

EACH me to do your will, for you are my God. Let your gracious Spirit lead me along a level path. —Ps 143:10

REFLECTION. We do God's will by avoiding sin. But how do we choose when there are so many good things we might do? Which ones would God prefer us to accomplish?

In addition to Jesus, God has given us the Spirit as our teacher in doing God's will. We open ourselves to His impulses by reading the Bible, receiving the Sacraments, and praying deeply.

PRAYER. *Holy Spirit, make me sensitive to Your movements in my heart and lead me today.*

UT of the mouths of newborn babes and infants you have brought forth praise as a bulwark against your foes. —Ps 8:3a

REFLECTION. As Jesus entered Jerusalem, the children acclaimed Him as the Son of David, but the chief priests and scribes became indignant. Those of little account often understand better than the more powerful.

When Jesus returns, He will vindicate the little ones and reward those who took care of the least of His brothers and sisters.

PRAYER. *O Lord, grant me the grace to appreciate and help those deemed insignificant by the world.*

DO NOT reject or forsake me, O God, my Savior. Even if my father and mother abandon me, the Lord will gather me up. —Ps 27:9b-10

AUG. 2

REFLECTION. God is the origin and model for all human parenthood. Yet, God's love surpasses the love of human parents and sustains us long after they precede us in death.

If our parents should ever stand in the way of our following Jesus, we must prefer Him; this is what He means that to be His disciples we must hate father or mother or relatives.

PRAYER. *O Jesus, help me to put You ahead of my family members when necessary.*

ASCRIBE to the Lord glory and might. Ascribe to the Lord the glory due to his name; worship the Lord in the splendor of his holiness. —Ps 29:1b-2

AUG. 3

REFLECTION. In loving trust, God has revealed Himself intimately to us. We come to know His power and love, His glory and holiness.

Our response can only be adoration and praise. What an injustice to use His name for other purposes! What a lack of gratitude not to praise Him!

PRAYER. *Almighty God, may I always honor You in my heart and with my lips.*

THE Lord has sworn, and he will not retract his oath: "You are a priest forever according to the order of Melchizedek."
—Ps 110:4

AUG. 4

REFLECTION. God insists on making one man a priest who will minister forever. This man is Jesus Christ, Who is also God's Son.

This special priest remains forever because God raised Him from the dead. Our earthly priests do not remain forever. All of them will die. Some will leave the active ministry. It is important to pray for our priests and to encourage and pray for vocations to the priesthood.

PRAYER. *O God, give the Church an abundance of faithful priests in the mold of Jesus.*

GAINST you, you alone, have I sinned; I have done what is evil in your sight. Therefore, you are right in accusing me and just in passing judgment.
—Ps 51:6

AUG. 5

REFLECTION. We hurt others when we choose to do wrong. While God cannot be hurt, every wrong we inflict on others is an offense against God.

Sins are acts contrary to God's commandments and hurt human beings whom God loves. So we must seek out not only others' forgiveness for our trespasses, but also God's pardon.

PRAYER. *Father, forgive me my trespasses against others.*

OOK to him and you will be radiant; your faces will never be covered with shame. —Ps 34:6

REFLECTION. Jesus' glory became visibly radiant at His transfiguration, and His glory was confirmed at His resurrection.

St. Paul explained, "It is God who said, 'Let light shine out of darkness,' that has shone into our hearts to enlighten them with the knowledge of God's glory, the glory on the face of Christ" (2 Cor 4:6).

PRAYER. *O God, we praise and thank You for the day when we will look upon the face of Christ with uncovered faces so that we may be transformed into the image of the Lord.*

T WAS there that your ancestors sought to tempt me; they put me to the test even though they had witnessed my works. —Ps 95:9

REFLECTION. To put God to the test is to doubt His love and power and to try to force Him to act. It is an attempt to control God, and it erodes the trust and respect that we should have for Him.

The Son of God refused to tempt or put God to the test. He let God the Father have control and did His will. God approved most highly of His Son Jesus.

PRAYER. *Lord God, help me never to doubt that Your control of my life is for my ultimate well-being.*

HEN my tongue shall proclaim your righteousness and sing your praise all the day long. **AUG. 8** —Ps 35:28

REFLECTION. Our mouths are constantly running. If we like something, we speak about it; and if don't, we speak even more.

The world needs designated preachers. Thank God for them! The world needs volunteer and occasional preachers as well. Let us beg God for them!

PRAYER. *O Lord, help me to stop boasting about myself and start boasting about You Who are all deserving of our praise.*

 O NOT place your trust in princes, in mortal men who have no power to save. When the spirit departs, they return to the earth; on that very day all their plans come to naught. **AUG. 9** —Ps 146:3-4

REFLECTION. We rely on others for many things, and rightly so. But no human being can help us always and in all ways. None can ultimately save us.

God is without equal in power and love, and He alone is worthy of ultimate trust. Those who put their faith in Him will not be disappointed.

PRAYER. *Saving God, may human weakness and frailty move me to rely on You to bring me from darkness to light.*

E BESTOWS gifts lavishly on the poor; his righteousness will endure forever, and his horn will be exalted in glory.
—Ps 112:9

AUG. 10

REFLECTION. Because people of faith view everything as a gift from God, they give as a gift what they have received as a gift.

God loves the cheerful giver, and He is pleased to bless them abundantly so that they may have enough for their needs and their resources may overflow into charitable works.

PRAYER. *Father, I thank you for Your providential goodness to me, and I ask You to help me to be generous to those in need.*

 AITHFULNESS will spring forth from the earth, and righteousness will look down from heaven.
—Ps 85:12

AUG. 11

REFLECTION. Earth shall reach up to heaven, and heaven shall reach down to earth. God and humankind will come together and be reconciled.

This hope was realized through Jesus and His disciples, even though the reconciliation is still incomplete. As we are reconciled to God, we are ambassadors for Christ and servants of reconciliation between God and the world.

PRAYER. *O Lord, reconcile us so that we may bring others closer to You.*

ONG ago You laid the foundations of the **AUG.** earth, and the heavens are the work of your hands. They will pass away but you endure; they will all wear out like a garment. . . . However, you remain always the same. —Ps 102:26-27a, 28a

AUG.

12

REFLECTION. Everything changes; everything passes away. Only God, the creator of all things, is eternal and unchangeable.

As God acted towards our ancestors so He acts towards us. God is constant—indeed, He is constancy itself—and thus the anchor of our fleeting lives.

PRAYER. *Almighty God, in the flux of life fix my attention and devotion on You.*

 AKE delight in the Lord, and he will **AUG.** grant you what your heart desires. Commit your way to the Lord; place your trust in him, and he will act. —Ps 37:4-5

AUG.

13

REFLECTION. A misunderstanding shared by many is that those who focus on God miss out on life. On the contrary, the Lord gives them what they truly desire and more.

Another common misconception is that we must work feverishly in order to succeed. Rather, the Lord acts powerfully in the lives of those who trust Him.

PRAYER. *Help me, O God, to be as the farmer who after much work waits with hope for the rain to make his efforts fruitful.*

HE earth is the Lord's and everything in it, the world and all who live in it.
—Ps 24:1

AUG. 14

REFLECTION. No matter what anyone might claim, the whole world is God's world, and He loves all of it. "God so loved the world. . . ."

Belonging to the Lord and being loved by Him, the world is the common possession of all God's children, who have the responsibility of caring for it and sharing its benefits with one another.

PRAYER. *Almighty God, help me to appreciate the grandeur of Your creation and to recognize all people as precious to You.*

 E RAISES the poor from the dust and lifts the needy from the rubbish heap, seating them with princes, with the princes of his people.
—Ps 113:7-8

AUG. 15

REFLECTION. God raised up the Patriarch Joseph, once a slave, to become the Pharaoh's chief minister. Jesus would teach that if not immediately, then eventually, God would compensate the poor, especially the poor in spirit.

The Virgin Mary understood this. And through her, God realized the exaltation of the poor in an utterly unique manner, that is, by assuming her, body and soul, into heaven.

PRAYER. *O God, may the example and prayers of the Virgin Mary help me to become humble.*

120

REMEMBER the word you gave to your servant by which you have given me hope. This is my consolation in my distress: your word gives me life. **AUG. 16**

—Ps 119:49-50

REFLECTION. When we "give our word" to others we make a promise or commitment. Our word is our pledge to them that we will follow through on our commitment.

At times we do not follow through, but God always does so, just as He fulfilled His promises in the Old Testament in Jesus. When life is difficult, it helps to remember God's promises.

PRAYER. *Lord God, revive all who are hopeless and lifeless by the word of Your promise.*

 "**T**HE poor have been oppressed, and those who are needy groan. Therefore, I will rise up now," says the Lord; "I will grant them the safety for which they long." **AUG. 17**

—Ps 12:6

REFLECTION. God is present to the suffering of the needy and oppressed even when their adversity continues for a long time. Eventually, God will intervene and grant relief, as in the case of Israel.

But if God is to rise up, the afflicted themselves must long for salvation and not lose hope. A reinforcement to such hope is the memory of Israel's history and the story of Jesus.

PRAYER. *O God, keep alive in me the memory of Your great deeds of the past.*

MY FRIENDS and companions stay away from my affliction, and my neighbors keep their distance.

AUG.
18

—Ps 38:12

REFLECTION. When we are suffering or have problems, we look for the company and support of friends and acquaintances. But when we need them most, they may not be found.

Jesus Himself experienced this, so He knows the added anguish it causes. Yet, He forgave His selfish and fearful disciples and made them His true friends by the gift of the Holy Spirit.

PRAYER. *O Lord, help me to be present to my friends in times of trouble, and grant me such faithful friends in turn.*

I SAY, "If only I had wings like a dove so that I could fly away and be at rest! . . . I would hurry to a place of refuge, far from the savage wind and tempest."

AUG.
19

—Ps 55:7, 9

REFLECTION. When difficulties increase, we wish we could simply leave them behind us and find rest elsewhere. But the dove from Noah's ark could not find a place to rest until God made the waters recede.

We would do better flying to the Lord in prayer, asking His intervention, and begging interior strength to tackle our problems and carry our burdens—until He should remove them.

PRAYER. *Almighty God, when the tempest rages all around me, give rest and peace to my soul.*

IKE arrows in the hands of a warrior are the children born in one's youth. Blessed is the man who has filled his quiver with them. —Ps 127:4-5

AUG. 20

REFLECTION. Children are costly. They cost their parents money, time, worry, leisure, and sleep. If they are costly, it is because they are also precious. They help parents to know themselves better and to go beyond themselves in love.

Children are the primordial investment. Most of them yield a profit in time, as they assist and support their parents in old age.

PRAYER. *Father, heal the hurt of all parents whose children have become not a help but a burden.*

 WILL instruct you and guide you in the way you should go; I will counsel you and keep my eyes upon you. Do not behave without understanding. —Ps 32:8-9a

AUG. 21

REFLECTION. As necessary as it was, none of us as children volunteered to go to school. This is because learning is often challenging and always work. It is easier not to learn.

But God gave all of us some capacity for learning, for to live without understanding is a sure recipe for a life poorly lived. Essential for a good life is to be taught by God.

PRAYER. *O Lord, help me to seek Your instruction for my life through the Church.*

T YOUR right hand is your queen adorned in gold of Ophir.

AUG. 22

—Ps 45:10b

REFLECTION. As the Incarnate Son Who was obedient to the Father's will unto death was exalted as Lord or King, so also His Mother who consented to the Father's plan was worthy of exaltation as our Lady or Queen.

Whoever wishes to be great will do so by becoming the servant of others. This is healthy Christian ambition.

PRAYER. *O Mary, as I claim you as my Queen, may I also live according to your example of humble service until God raises me high, as He did you.*

_____

 UT they have all turned aside; all alike are corrupt. There is no one who does what is right, not even one.

AUG. 23

—Ps 53:4

REFLECTION. Sin is universal. All are sinners—with the exception of Jesus and of His Blessed Mother. Humankind's sad state is precisely why God provided us with the Savior.

It is wrong to see others as sinners and ourselves as righteous and on this basis to condemn everyone but ourselves. If we want to receive God's mercy, we must ask God's forgiveness for our sins.

PRAYER. *O God, show me my sins and help me to embrace fellow sinners with compassion.*

THE Lord is righteous in all his ways and merciful in everything he does. The Lord is near to all who call out to him, to all who call out to him sincerely.

AUG. 24

—Ps 145:17-18

REFLECTION. Jesus remarked about the forthright Nathanael or Bartholomew that he was a man without deception. God appreciates sincerity.

We are at our sincerest or most truthful when we acknowledge our sins, limitations, and needs and cry out for God's mercy and help. Am I in touch with the truth of my abilities and limits?

PRAYER. *O Lord, I praise You for Your generous mercy which enables me to be honest with You and myself.*

_____

YOURS is the day, and yours also is the night, for you set in place both sun and moon.

AUG. 25

—Ps 74:16

REFLECTION. When God created light, He also allowed darkness to have its time. Yet, even then, He gave to the night the flicker of the moon in order to remind us of the greater light of the sun.

At times God allows darkness to descend over us. Yet, because of Jesus' victory over sin and death, we are never without hope. And the darkness will eventually give way to God's light.

PRAYER. *Almighty God, grant me confidence in Your ability to make all things work together for my good.*

125

THE plan of the Lord remains forever, the designs of his heart for all generations. **AUG. 26**

—Ps 33:11

REFLECTION. Our plans are constantly changing not just because we can't manage to accomplish them but because our hearts desire now this thing and then that thing.

God's plan does not change precisely because His desires are always the same: to love and save all people. Paradoxically, human resistance to God ensures His pursuit of the same plan for all generations.

PRAYER. *O Lord, may all my desires and plans be fixed on You.*

THE Lord has heard the sound of my weeping. The Lord has listened to my pleas; the Lord has accepted my prayer. **AUG. 27**

—Ps 6:9b-10

REFLECTION. Our tears indicate that what has been lost was precious to us. Jesus wept over the loss of His friend Lazarus. God is not indifferent to our weeping.

Do we weep in our prayer, as did St. Monica for her errant son? If not, perhaps we are not completely sincere about what we're requesting in prayer.

PRAYER. *Jesus, help me to feel deeply and to request shamelessly, for You, too, know what it is to cry.*

LORD, all my longing is known to you, and my sighs are not hidden from you.
—Ps 38:10

AUG. 28

REFLECTION. As our desires outstrip what we have, we may feel frustrated, but we do not cease to seek fulfillment. This all too common experience leads us to suspect that we will never be satisfied.

But the experience of the saints indicates otherwise. St. Augustine exclaimed, "Our hearts are restless, until they rest in You, O Lord."

PRAYER. *Father, You know my deepest longings better than I do. Help me to seek You and to find in You complete satisfaction.*

 HAVE relied upon you since birth, and you have been my strength from my mother's womb; my praise rises unceasingly to you.
—Ps 71:6

AUG. 29

REFLECTION. From the womb the Baptist acknowledged Jesus; and to defend the Truth, John went to his tomb.

God made none of us for death. As He willed our being in the womb and our coming forth from it into life, He will also allow our going into the tomb and then act to bring us forth to life.

PRAYER. *O God, because we are precious to You, we do not fear death. Fill us with childlike wonder so that we may praise You every day as You deserve.*

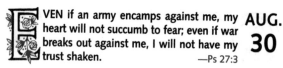 VEN if an army encamps against me, my heart will not succumb to fear; even if war breaks out against me, I will not have my trust shaken. **AUG. 30** —Ps 27:3

REFLECTION. Armies kill and wars destroy. There is neither denying nor minimizing this. But we know that God will eventually triumph as He was victorious over Jesus' executioners.

Our eternal salvation is not jeopardized by the evil others commit, unless we let ourselves be shaken by it and resort to evil ourselves.

PRAYER. *O God, when I am confronted by evil, dispel my fears by increasing my trust in You.*

 E SENT forth his word and healed them, saving them from the grave. Let them give thanks to the Lord for his kindness and for the wonders he does for people. **AUG. 31** —Ps 107:20-21

REFLECTION. God sent forth His Word Made Flesh in Jesus. He healed the sick by His word, and so saved many from the grave. He will eventually save His faithful from the grave by having us rise from there.

Because of this, we thank God. But we also announce to others the good news so that they may be healed by Jesus now and be raised with us from the grave.

PRAYER. *Lord God, Your kindness surpasses all bounds; may our praise of You reach the ends of the earth.*

AY the glory of the Lord abide forever, and may the Lord rejoice in his works. —Ps 104:31

REFLECTION. When God created the world, He found joy in His works—especially in humankind—but His joy was blocked by their sin.

God's glory appeared in the world in Christ so that it might transform men and women from glory into glory. Thus His glory abides again on earth and gives God great joy.

PRAYER. *Lord, may the vision of Your glory transform me so that You might rejoice over me.*

HEY say, "The Lord does not see; the God of Jacob pays no attention." Does the one who made the ear not hear? Does the one who fashioned the eye not see? —Ps 94:7, 9

REFLECTION. We tend to behave better when we're conscious of being observed. But the fact is that we are always being watched by God, not so that He might catch us misbehaving, but so as to guard us.

Under God's gaze, we should live with integrity—doing and saying what is right and just—to please Him.

PRAYER. *Father, may I see myself under Your loving gaze and through Your discerning eyes.*

E REACHED down from on high and snatched me up; he drew me out of the watery depths. —Ps 18:17

SEPT. 3

REFLECTION. When we go swimming, we hope never to need a lifeguard. But if we get into trouble, we are happy to have one come to our rescue. Such is our God.

From time to time, we begin to drown under the waves of life's difficulties. If we call out to the Lord, as Peter called out to Jesus to save him, He will reach down and snatch us up so that we may not perish.

PRAYER. *Lord Jesus, save me when adversity threatens to engulf me.*

 ET the words of my mouth and the thoughts of my heart find favor in Your sight, O Lord, my Rock and my Redeemer. —Ps 19:15

SEPT. 4

REFLECTION. Words are the shell of the seed, and thoughts are its kernel. Both are necessary. A seed whose shell looks healthy, but whose kernel is rotted, is useless. So also is the case with our words.

Because God knows us thoroughly, we ask Him to give us kind and uplifting words as well as hearts filled with love and appreciation for Him and for ourselves and our neighbors.

PRAYER. *O Lord, transform my words and thoughts so that they may be worthy of You.*

130

CRY aloud to God, for when I cry out to God, he hears me. In the time of my distress I seek the Lord. —Ps 77:2-3a

REFLECTION. If prayer is being present to God, then we must go about it thoughtfully, that is, not with empty words. Our voices give fuller expression to our desires and expectations.

The Son of God called out to the Father with loud cries and tears, and He was heard by God Who raised Him from the dead.

PRAYER. *Father, help me to cry out to You as I once cried out to my parents.*

 EOPLE go forth to their work and to their labor until darkness descends. —Ps 104:23

REFLECTION. Jesus said to His disciples that they must do the work of God while it was still day, for the night was approaching when no one could work.

Work has its place in the rhythm of life. It is not an insignificant part of life, but neither should it overtake our lives. This is a matter for our personal and prayerful consideration.

PRAYER. *Lord God, help me to work, play, and rest according to Your will.*

LORD, you are kind and forgiving, filled with kindness for all who cry to you.
—Ps 86:5

SEPT. 7

REFLECTION. God is kind and always ready to forgive, like the father in the parable of the Prodigal Son. Yet God's forgiveness can be secured only if we seek it, as the young son did in the same parable.

If we behave like the older son or like the Pharisees, we will wallow in our sins.

PRAYER. *Loving Father, overcoming pride and sloth, I beg Your forgiveness; grant it in Your kindness.*

 WAS entrusted to your care at my birth; from my mother's womb you have been my God.
—Ps 22:11

SEPT. 8

REFLECTION. An ancient tradition tells us that Saints Joachim and Anne raised Mary in the ways of piety and placed her in service to the Temple at an early age, as Elkanah and Hannah did with Samuel.

Many children grow up in the faith; others do not. Parents, grandparents, and godparents are especially called to do all they can to ensure that the Lord is the God of our young.

PRAYER. *Lord, I thank You for the precious gift of faith. Help me to pass it on.*

OU listen, O Lord, to the longings of the poor; you strengthen their courage and heed their prayers. —Ps 10:17

REFLECTION. Even before the poor and downtrodden pray to Him, the Lord knows their longings; then He answers their prayers and fills them with hope.

Would that we were as attentive and responsive! Like the rich man in Luke's Gospel, we often pay little attention to poor Lazarus at our door. But we can choose to do otherwise.

PRAYER. *Open my eyes and my heart, O Lord, to notice and respond to those in need.*

 E HAS no fear of bad news, for his heart remains steadfast, trusting in the Lord. Since his heart is tranquil, he will not be afraid. . . . —Ps 112:7-8a

REFLECTION. Sometimes bad news hits close to home. It is natural to be afraid when we consider our vulnerability and limitations. Walking on the sea, St. Peter began to sink when he encountered the wind.

The key is to look beyond our problems to God. If we trust in Him, then our fears will diminish, and we'll be able to navigate life's disturbances safely.

PRAYER. *O God, keep the eyes of my heart fixed steadily on You through all the storms of life.*

HEN I look up at your heavens that have been formed by your fingers, the moon and the stars that you set in place, what is man that you are mindful of him.

SEPT. 11

—Ps 8:4-5a

REFLECTION. Our galaxy is only one of about 200 billion galaxies. To count the stars in our galaxy alone would take about 2,500 years.

The immensity of creation fills us with wonder at the greatness of God and of His immense love. Only love can explain why God chose to make men and women in His image and likeness and ultimately to become one of us.

PRAYER. *Mighty God, may the evidence of Your greatness move me to heartfelt worship.*

LESS the Lord, O my soul; my entire being, bless his holy name. —Ps 103:1

SEPT. 12

REFLECTION. The name of God is holy or special. To bless God's name is to speak well of God, to praise Him. Echoing this psalm, Mary did just this in her *Magnificat*.

Elizabeth blessed Mary, who then prophesied that all generations would call her blessed. Mary's name, too, is holy. To praise Mary is to honor God Who chose and graced her.

PRAYER. *O God, I am grateful for what you have done through Mary. Help me to revere and invoke her name.*

MY MOUTH will speak words of wisdom, and the utterance of my heart will give understanding. —Ps 49:4

SEPT. 13

All of us have spoken words that we later regretted. Thus, it is difficult to see how these words of the psalmist fit us.

But they can if we seek to learn from them. God has not been stingy in providing wise people throughout history to enlighten and correct us.

PRAYER. *Holy Spirit, give me wisdom and an understanding heart to speak what is true.*

NOW I know that the Lord will grant victories to his anointed; he will answer him from his holy heaven. —Ps 20:7a

SEPT. 14

REFLECTION. God granted to His Son, Whom He had anointed with the Spirit, victory over His enemies, the Cross, and death. As Jesus' disciples, we too have been anointed with the Spirit.

Those who gain victory over evil are precisely those who believe in Jesus and live by faith in Him. Today is a good day to request earnestly an increase in this gift.

PRAYER. *Almighty God, we believe. Help our unbelief. Increase our faith.*

HOW great is your goodness, O Lord, which you have stored up for those who fear you, and which you bestow on those who take refuge in you in the presence of all the people. —Ps 31:20

REFLECTION. We do not at all times experience God's goodness; often it is stored up, as it was for Jesus, the Lord's Suffering Servant, and for Mary, our Lady of Sorrows.

In the face of troubles, we remember God's promise through Jeremiah: "I will turn their mourning into joy; I will console and gladden them after their sorrows."

PRAYER. *O Lord, although we must undergo many hardships to enter Your kingdom, remind me that You are my refuge and strength.*

THEN I will go to the altar of God, to the God of my joy and delight. —Ps 43:4a

REFLECTION. To spend our money on a gift for someone we love deeply is no burden, for that person gives us joy. Similarly, to spend our time, energy, and resources at God's altar is no burden, for God gives us joy.

The Lord fills us with joy by the many ways He shows us His love, for example, His providence and forgiveness.

PRAYER. *O God, move me to participate in Mass as though it were a party for a dear friend.*

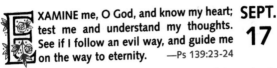 XAMINE me, O God, and know my heart; **SEPT.** test me and understand my thoughts. See if I follow an evil way, and guide me on the way to eternity. —Ps 139:23-24 **17**

REFLECTION. We do not enjoy taking tests, whether medical or scholastic. But without the diagnosis or evaluation they provide, our health or learning can be jeopardized. Thus, the psalmist wisely invites God to test him.

God knows us better than we know ourselves. And when He reveals to us our hearts, He also guides us to healing and holiness.

PRAYER. *Lord, may I see my heart clearly through Your compassionate and forgiving eyes.*

 OW countless are your works, O **SEPT.** Lord; by your wisdom you have made them all; the earth abounds with your creatures. —Ps 104:24 **18**

REFLECTION. To the present day humankind has not been able to discover and catalogue all God's creatures on earth. Their vast number is a small reflection of the awesome power and love of God.

An even greater number of God's "works" consists of what God accomplishes in the life of every man and woman. And always He works so that all may be saved and experience the fullness of life.

PRAYER. *Lord God, grant me the vision to see and appreciate Your works in my life.*

137

AS FAR as the east is from the west, so far has he removed our transgressions from us. —Ps 103:12

REFLECTION. Not everything we acquire is good. Or if it once was, it breaks down or in time it looks old and tired. So we get rid of the clutter and throw out the trash.

Not everything we do is good; this is sin or transgression. God has acted to remove humankind's "trash" by means of Jesus, and He does so for each disciple in the Sacrament of Penance.

PRAYER. *As I get rid of clutter, O God, help me to be rid of my sins by going to Confession.*

BEHOLD, he who conceives iniquity and is pregnant with mischief will give birth to lies. . . . His wickedness will recoil upon his own head, and his violence will fall back on his own crown. —Ps 7:15, 17

REFLECTION. It is better to suffer for doing what is right than to suffer for doing evil. For while evil may bring momentary comfort to evildoers, it will hurt them in the end.

But doing right brings blessings. At the very least, it preserves us in our God-given integrity. Think of Cain and Abel. The truly tragic figure was Cain, the evildoer, not the innocent victim Abel.

PRAYER. *O Lord, help all evildoers to choose what is right and to spare the innocent.*

MY HEART is moved by a noble theme as I sing my poem to the king; my tongue is like the pen of a skillful scribe. —Ps 45:2

**SEPT.
21**

REFLECTION. What is in the heart eventually makes its way to the tongue. If we focus our hearts on a noble theme, then what will issue from our mouths will likewise be gracious.

The evangelists spoke about the noblest theme of all: Jesus. They aimed to present not only the facts about Him, but Jesus Himself. Their works are manifestations of love for Him.

PRAYER. *O God, fill my heart with the noblest theme, Jesus, and let me speak of Him with wisdom and with love.*

YOUR words are sweet to my palate, even sweeter to my tongue than honey. Through your commandments I achieve wisdom; therefore, I hate every way that is false. —Ps 119:103-104

**SEPT.
22**

REFLECTION. God's word is good news. God loves us not because we're good, but because He is good. And because He loves us, He wants us to become the best that we can be.

Jesus preached the good news of God's approaching kingdom, and in view of it He called for repentance. He came to help us to be true to His word and work in us.

PRAYER. *Lord Jesus, may I savor Your word both when it is sweet and when it is tart.*

THEY have mouths but they cannot speak; they have eyes but they cannot see. They have ears but they cannot hear. . . . Those who make them end up like them, as do all who place their trust in them. —Ps 115:5-6a, 8

REFLECTION. Ancient people used to worship idols that could never deliver on their hopes because they were non-living things even less capable than the humans who served them.

In our search for happiness, we may pour all our efforts into our careers or property. These things cannot bring us happiness, and we become less than human by serving them.

PRAYER. *Almighty God, help me to see and renounce my modern-day idols.*

IN TIME of good fortune, I said, "Nothing can ever sway me." O Lord, in your goodness you established me as an impregnable mountain; however, when you hid your face, I was filled with terror. —Ps 30:7-8

REFLECTION. It is an all too common mistake to assume in good times that we are responsible for our success. Eventual misfortune helps us to see that we gave ourselves too much credit.

When success vanishes, we gain humility and wisdom. We learn to thank God in good times and seek His help in bad times.

PRAYER. *O God, as we strive to succeed, let us acknowledge our need for Your blessing.*

THEY still will bear fruit, in their old age, and they will remain fresh and green. —Ps 92:15

REFLECTION. The psalmist is not speaking about plants or trees; rather, he is comparing righteous people to these. Though the righteous get old, as do sinners, the righteous remain vibrant and fruitful.

This is because the faithful draw their nourishment from God, the source of all life, and with God's grace they are able to pass it on to others.

PRAYER. *O God, make me alive and vibrant with Your love so that I may be fruitful and help others to grow.*

LET integrity and virtue preserve me, for in you I place my hope. —Ps 25:21

REFLECTION. The Lord is good, just, and virtuous. Yet our world is full of evil, injustice, and violence, and those who are good may find it hard to remain so.

If we place our hope in the Lord, the origin and destiny of all things, then we shall persist in integrity and virtue.

PRAYER. *O Lord, guard me from doubt and cynicism and fill me with joy and peace.*

RANT justice to the weak and the orphan; defend the rights of the lowly and the poor. —Ps 82:3

REFLECTION. God Himself is the father of orphans and the defender of widows. What happens to the vulnerable does not ultimately depend on us, but it does not let us off the hook either.

As children imitate their parents, we imitate God—or at least we should. It is our prerogative and our glory to do as God does and to advance His kingdom.

PRAYER. *Almighty God, I accept your invitation to cooperate with You in caring for the most vulnerable.*

———————

 HESE things we have heard and know, for our ancestors have related them to us. We will not conceal them from our children; we will relate them to the next generation, the glorious and powerful deeds of the Lord. —Ps 78:3-4a

REFLECTION. All human progress requires education. Privileged to be educated as children, we are right to ensure that the next generation be educated in turn.

Vital to this education is knowledge of God, His deeds, and His ways; for to be unschooled in God is to be ignorant of where we have come from and where we are going.

PRAYER. *Assist me, Almighty God, to pass on knowledge of You and Your saving ways.*

BLESS the Lord, O you his angels, you mighty in strength who do his bidding, who obey his spoken word. —Ps 103:20 **SEPT. 29**

REFLECTION. Though mighty in strength, God's Angels and Archangels do not use their power to do what they please, but what pleases God.

Though lower than the Angels, we have the ability to accomplish much good in the world. Do I seek out what God wants done through me and ask the Angels to assist me?

PRAYER. *Almighty God, help me to bear hardships for the sake of the Gospel with the strength that comes from You and the Angels.*

THE explanation of your words gives light and imparts understanding to the simple. —Ps 119:130 **SEPT. 30**

REFLECTION. As young students we read words that we recognized but did not make sense to us at that time. The same can be true of God's word in the Bible.

A clear instance is the Ethiopian officer in Acts 8 who could not understand the words of Isaiah until Philip explained their significance. We, too, need competent teachers to guide us.

PRAYER. *O God, I thank You for all those who teach the Catholic faith. Continue to help them and me to understand and explain Your word.*

HAVE stilled and calmed my soul, hushed it like a weaned child. Like a weaned child held in its mother's arms, so is my soul within me. —Ps 131:2

OCT. 1

REFLECTION. When we are young, we cannot wait to grow up; then, we tell ourselves, we can do what we want and be happy. When we are older, we realize that we were only half right: although we do as we want, we are not always happier.

Jesus taught that if we would enter God's kingdom and share His happiness, we must become as little children who know and do what the Father wants.

PRAYER. *Lord Jesus, help me to find joy in doing the Father's will, just as You did.*

 E WILL command his angels about you—to guard you wherever you go. —Ps 91:11

OCT. 2

REFLECTION. God sent an Angel to guard Israel on the way to the Promised Land, just as He later would send Raphael to be with Tobiah on his way to Media and back. The Lord's Angel protects and delivers God's faithful ones.

Yet we may not presume on this gift of God's goodness by putting ourselves in harm's way. Jesus taught us this when He resisted the devil's temptations to jump from the Temple.

PRAYER. *Father, we are grateful for the ministering spirits whom You send to serve us.*

144

HE Lord of hosts is with us; the God of Jacob is our fortress. Come and behold the works of the Lord, the astonishing deeds he has wrought on the earth. —Ps 46:8-9

REFLECTION. When we live in security and abundance, it may be easy to affirm that God is with us. But it's not easy when blessings are scarce.

In order that He might be with us in a constant and fuller way, God became a man in Jesus, Who is God *with* Us. At His ascension, Jesus promised, "Behold, I am with You always. . . ."

PRAYER. *Lord, may Your presence in the Church, the Sacraments, and the word sustain me in difficult times.*

 LL your creatures praise you, O Lord, and all your saints bless you. They relate the glory of your kingdom and tell of all your power. —Ps 145:10-11

REFLECTION. The beauty of the natural world gives silent praise to God the Creator. We ourselves are part of creation; and as St. Francis intuited, the sun is our brother and the moon is our sister.

Because we have mouths, we can voice our praise of God—or not. By our words and deeds, we can choose to bless God—or not. The right choice is ours to make.

PRAYER. *O Lord, fill my heart and mouth with gratitude for all Your gifts, especially nature.*

WILL not violate my covenant or alter the promise I have spoken. "By my holiness I have sworn once and for all: never will I break faith with David." —Ps 89:35-36

OCT. 5

REFLECTION. What a guarantee! God promised never to break His commitment to David, which was that a descendant of His would rule over Israel and the nations.

In faithfulness to this covenant, God made His Son Jesus to be born of Mary, espoused to Joseph of the house of David. God anointed Jesus the Messiah or Christ.

PRAYER. *O God, every time I call Jesus "Christ" remind me of Your fidelity to Your covenant and make me faithful to You.*

 UT I make my appeal to God, and the Lord will save me. Evening, morning, and noon I will cry out in my distress, and he will hear my voice. —Ps 55:17-18

OCT. 6

REFLECTION. When a purchase is not what we expected, we contact the manufacturer's customer service department. When life is problematic, there is Someone with Whom we can file our appeal.

If we place our petition with God, more than satisfaction is guaranteed, for when Jesus put in His appeal with the Father He got the glorified life of the resurrection.

PRAYER. *Father, grant me faith to believe You will respond perfectly to my prayers.*

WILL remember the works of the Lord. . . . **OCT.**
I will reflect on all your deeds and ponder **7**
your wondrous works.   —Ps 77:12a, 13

REFLECTION. Mary understood the events of her life as ordained by God. She reflected on them and pondered His prodigious works.

As we pray the Rosary of the Blessed Virgin Mary, we too reflect on God's deeds of the past and we learn to trust His present action in both the joyful and sorrowful times of life.

PRAYER. *Jesus, we thank You for giving us Your Mother to be our own. Help us to imitate her in faith-filled meditation on the events of Your life.*

 HE Lord will not abandon his people **OCT.**
or forsake his heritage.   —Ps 94:14 **8**

REFLECTION. The Church is God's special possession or heritage in the world. There are periods when the Church falters because of the collective and grievous sins of her members.

Although we may be unfaithful, the Lord remains faithful. When He lets hardship visit His people, we come to realize that His discipline is also a sign of His fidelity.

PRAYER. *Lord Jesus, restore and renew Your people that the world might believe in You.*

HE way of God is blameless, and the Lord's promise proves true; he is a shield to all who flee to him for safety. —Ps 18:31

OCT. 9

REFLECTION. We spend our days blaming or assigning credit. Most often we take credit for ourselves; sometimes we give credit to others; frequently we blame others. Now and again we blame God.

Because God gave us free will, He should not be blamed when human beings act against His law or will. If He were obeyed more often, the world would be in much better shape.

PRAYER. *Help me, O Lord, to stop pointing the finger of blame at others or You.*

 FFER thanksgiving as you enter his gates, sing hymns of praise as you approach his courts; give thanks to him and bless his name. —Ps 100:4

OCT. 10

REFLECTION. In our time, cathedrals are filled with crowds of tourists. But the worshipers are few. Polls reveal that the failure to worship stems not from doubt, but from forgetfulness.

We've forgotten the Gospel that inspired what's best in the world, and we've forgotten the Lord Who has brought us through the most violent century to relative peace and prosperity in our day.

PRAYER. *Almighty God, thank You for Your abundant blessings that never cease.*

148

I N YOUR abundant compassion wipe away my offenses. Wash me completely from my guilt, and cleanse me from my sin.
—Ps 51:3b-4

REFLECTION. Even when we truly believe in God's mercy and goodness, we find it difficult to let go of the guilt we carry. The psalmist asks God for just such a thorough cleansing of himself from sin.

God has provided the means for this in the blood Jesus spilled on the Cross. Through sacramental absolution, we receive God's forgiveness and the grace to forgive ourselves.

PRAYER. *O God, by sacramental grace, rid me completely of the defilement of sin.*

D O NOT fret over the man who prospers because of his evil schemes. Refrain from anger and turn away from wrath; do not fret—it does nothing but harm.
—Ps 37:7b-8

REFLECTION. Anger is appropriate as an emotional response to injustice. Mark's gospel tells us that Jesus Himself grew angry, but He did not let His anger dictate His actions.

Untamed anger is destructive of ourselves first of all and then of others to whom it closes the door to reconciliation.

PRAYER. *O Lord, channel my justifiable anger by means of Your love and mercy.*

YOU are the most handsome of men; grace has anointed your lips, for God has blessed you forever. —Ps 45:3

OCT. 13

REFLECTION. Many were attracted to Jesus at the outset and admired Him throughout His ministry, because of the gracious words that came forth from His mouth.

Jesus condemned no one, but offered all forgiveness and encouragement to repentance: "Neither do I condemn you; go, and do not sin again."

PRAYER. *Lord, as I have benefited by Your gracious forgiveness, help me to extend it to others.*

 THE righteous will flourish like the palm tree; they will grow like a cedar of Lebanon. They are planted in the house of the Lord and will flourish in the courts of our God. —Ps 92:13-14

OCT. 14

REFLECTION. We all want to flourish. But who will truly flourish? And how? By being planted in God's house, which is the Church, through which we are given what we need: community, connection to God, Jesus' gifts.

If the Church has this God-given function, then we cannot afford simply to dabble in Church life; we must root ourselves there.

PRAYER. *Lord God, grant me to see the Church as my true home.*

SAY to the Lord, "You are my Lord; I have no good apart from you." —Ps 16:2

REFLECTION. The world is full of good things, and we have our share of these. Living in a consumer culture we get fixated on these goods and forget the good God Who is their source.

Our constant buying indicates that we are never satisfied by these goods. This then should lead us to the conclusion of St. Teresa of Avila that only God suffices, for He alone is the ultimate good.

PRAYER. *O Lord, You alone suffice. Help me to avoid the distractions of lesser goods.*

EAR my prayer, O Lord, and listen to my voice in supplication. In the time of trouble I call to you, for you will answer me. —Ps 86:6-7

REFLECTION. Our life is God's gift, as is everything else which we hold dear. All has been loaned to us by God.

Perhaps Jesus responded most readily to beggars in His path because they grasped that they were reliant on God and others. Knowing this will set us free.

PRAYER. *Almighty God, help me to recognize and rejoice in my reliance on You Who are so generous.*

T IS for your sake that I endure reproach and that shame covers my face. —Ps 69:8 **OCT. 17**

REFLECTION. It is good for us to feel guilt and be repentant when we are reproached by good people for doing wrong things.

And if we are confronted for doing what is right by people who are opposed to goodness, then we share Christ's lot.

PRAYER. *Almighty God, help me to discover Your grace in the opposition I meet for being a Christian.*

———————

 HEY make known to all people your mighty deeds and the glorious majesty of your kingdom. —Ps 145:12 **OCT. 18**

REFLECTION. St. Paul, announced the good news broadly to Jews and Gentiles, finally he proclaimed Jesus and the kingdom in Rome, the hub of ancient civilization.

The Apostles and evangelists announced the events that God accomplished in their midst, and we also are called to broadcast both those events and what God is still accomplishing among us and through us.

PRAYER. *Lord Jesus, I thank You for making me Your disciple. Help me to be also Your witness to all I meet.*

F THE Lord had not been on our side when our enemies attacked us, then they would have swallowed us alive. —Ps 124:2-3a

OCT. 19

REFLECTION. Beaten and battered, Israel could still recognize God's help. The Lord's help does not mean that we shall not experience suffering but that we shall emerge better on the other side of it.

If God is for us, who can be against us? Many are! But they will not prevail, any more than they ultimately prevailed over Jesus.

PRAYER. *Lord Jesus, when I am under attack for being Your disciple, help me to be victorious by means of Your love.*

 O NOT cast me off in my old age; do not forsake me when my strength is completely spent. —Ps 71:9

OCT. 20

REFLECTION. We throw away many items when they are no longer useful to us. To God, we are not disposable. He created each of us with an immortal soul.

As we age, we can be thoughtful and kind even when our bodies are less able. And when we are too old even for this, we can devote ourselves to ceaseless prayer.

PRAYER. *Father, teach me to age well, that is, in Your will and grace.*

YOUR word is a lamp for my feet and a light to my path. —Ps 119:105

REFLECTION. In a power outage, a flashlight can be a lifesaver. In the darkness of a world that is beset by evil, God's word is like a flashlight that lights a sure path.

God's Word became flesh in Jesus, Who is the Light of the World. In His light, we ourselves are changed to become light for others.

PRAYER. *O God, help me to own my light-producing role in the world and give me a greater attachment to Your word.*

 BUT Israel he would feed with the finest of wheat and fill them with honey from the rock. —Ps 81:17

REFLECTION. God fed Israel in the desert, and now He also feeds us, His new people in Christ, as we pass through the desert of the world to the kingdom of heaven.

By Christ's sacrifice on Calvary, we get to eat the finest wheat, Jesus Himself in the Eucharist. In this way, God also fills us with honey from the rock, because the Eucharist helps us to find the sweetness of God's love in life's hard experiences.

PRAYER. *O my Jesus, sustain and strengthen me with Your heavenly food until I reach Your kingdom.*

GRANT us your help against our enemies, for any human assistance is worthless. With God's help we will be victorious, for he will overwhelm our foes. —Ps 60:13-14

REFLECTION. This is the prayer of a people at war. It acknowledges that the most important ally—indeed, the only necessary one—is God.

But God will be our ally only if we are truly His friends too. This is to say that our cause must be just rather than selfish. And all other means must have been tried and failed.

PRAYER. *Lord God, may our wars and our conduct of them be just in Your sight.*

AS FOR me, I trust in your kindness; my heart rejoices in your salvation. I will sing to the Lord because he has been good to me. —Ps 13:6-7

REFLECTION. Emotionally unstable people laugh or cry without reason. Everyone else needs something or someone to make them laugh or cry, rejoice or grieve.

Without any obligation to save us, God does so. Though He could justifiably repay us for our sins, He is good to us. God's goodness is the reason for our rejoicing in song.

PRAYER. *Loving Father, may the kindness and goodness You show us lead us to praise You.*

RISE, O Lord! Lift up your hand, O God! Do not forget the afflicted. Why should the wicked reject God and say in his heart, "He will not call me to account"? —Ps 10:12-13

OCT. 25

REFLECTION. Those who flagrantly flaunt God's law by abusing others, reject God as He has revealed Himself. They think Him unjust or insufficiently powerful to deal with their wickedness.

They mistake His patience for injustice or weakness, whereas His patience is the opportunity He affords them to repent.

PRAYER. *O God, may the wicked see and seize the opportunity to repent and turn their lives to good.*

———————

 EACH me your ways, O Lord, so that I may walk in your truth. —Ps 86:11a

OCT. 26

REFLECTION. It is a point of pride with many people to be able to claim, "I did it my way." They have set aside others' counsel and forged their own way. We may need to rethink this as far as God is concerned.

The One Who is "the Way" was humble enough to do it God's way, to do only and always what God wanted. Through prayer and the Sacraments, we are able to do as Jesus did.

PRAYER. *Lord, "turn my eyes away from what is unimportant, and let me live in Your way" (Ps 119:37).*

HEN I call upon you, answer me, O God, you who uphold my rights. —Ps 4:2a

REFLECTION. Human dignity is the basis for human rights, and the foundation for human dignity is God's unique creation of us in His image and likeness. God establishes our rights.

God also upholds them in the face of those who violate them. He raises up prophets and leaders who defend and promote human rights.

PRAYER. *Almighty God, help me to treat everyone with dignity, even the wicked and abusive.*

 HE firmament shows forth the work of his hands. One day imparts that message to the next, and night conveys that knowledge to night. —Ps 19:2b-3

REFLECTION. The natural world exhibits God's existence and power. This truth should not be missed, but often it is. Therefore, God spoke through His prophets, and then He spoke directly and showed Himself in Jesus.

Because Jesus did not want to manifest Himself only to a few, His disciples spread word of Him. Very little is known of Jesus' first emissaries because they preached Jesus and not themselves.

PRAYER. *O Lord, teach us to speak only about You and never to boast about ourselves.*

O NOT fume because of evildoers or envy those who do wrong. They will wither quickly like the grass and fade away like the green herb. —Ps 37:1-2

REFLECTION. Because we try to do what is right, we are irate when we see unjust people thrive or we burn with envy at their success.

God throws water on our fire while withholding it from the wicked. So they shrivel up for lack of moisture whereas we are irrigated by God's peaceful Spirit.

PRAYER. *Eternal God, help me to leave the judgment of evildoers to you and to pray for their innocent victims.*

 UT you, O Lord, are a shield to protect me; you are my glory and the one who raises my head high. —Ps 3:4

REFLECTION. God may not protect us from physical harm any more than He did Jesus. But He will shield us from spiritual harm, as with Jesus, by keeping us from responding to evil with evil and so compromising our spiritual core.

If we conduct ourselves like Jesus, we shall be able to raise our heads high at His coming.

PRAYER. *O God, even now hold my head high before those who mock my fidelity to You.*

BLESSED be the Lord, my Rock, who trains my hands for war and my fingers for battle. —Ps 144:1

OCT. 31

REFLECTION. God trains His people, His soldiers, for spiritual warfare. But as St. Paul taught us, we are not contending against human enemies but against the spirits of darkness that inspire the wicked.

Against these we don the helmet of salvation, the sword of the Spirit, and breastplate of faith, and we train ourselves in righteousness and love.

PRAYER. *O Lord, increase my faith to believe that I can overcome evil with good.*

 LET the heavens praise your wonders, O Lord, your faithfulness in the assembly of your holy ones. —Ps 89:6

NOV. 1

REFLECTION. The Lord is surrounded in heaven not only by His Angels, but also by the saints, those who lived holy lives and await the resurrection. They intercede for us with God.

They also constitute that great cloud of witnesses to Jesus and to what we can become through grace. With their encouragement, we set aside every distraction to winning the race.

PRAYER. *Almighty God, I thank You for the example and prayers of the saints; with their help, make me fit for heaven.*

Y SOUL thirsts for God, the living God. When shall I come to behold the face of God? —Ps 42:3

REFLECTION. Whereas the gods of other religions are imaginary, the Lord truly exists. Indeed, He is the source of life: the living God. Because He lives, we live now and shall live eternally.

Some of the dead already enjoy living in God's presence; others wait and hope for this. They can be helped by our prayers and sacrifices.

PRAYER. *O God, speedily grant to all the dead the vision of Your gracious countenance.*

 CCLAIM the Lord with joy, all the earth; serve the Lord with gladness; enter his presence with songs of joy. —Ps 100:1-2

REFLECTION. Jesus said that He wished that His joy might be in His disciples. He rejoiced to find God's lost sheep, and heaven rejoiced with Him. Since God Himself is joyful, He wants us to be joyful as well.

Joy should characterize our service of God in worship and in our outreach to our neighbors. "Come share your master's joy!"

PRAYER. *O Lord, remove from my heart and my face all sadness and gloom so that others may know Your joy.*

Y INIQUITIES tower far above my head; they are a burden too heavy to bear. —Ps 38:5

REFLECTION. When traveling by plane, some passengers' baggage may be temporarily or forever lost. On the bright side, "leaving our baggage behind" can be quite beneficial.

Our sins and our sinful inclinations are heavy baggage. The Sacrament of Penance relieves us of our sins, and earnest prayer and the Eucharist can reduce the force of our sinful tendencies.

PRAYER. *Almighty God, by Your grace take from me any baggage that weighs me down.*

 HE Lord is my shepherd; there is nothing I shall lack. He makes me lie down in green pastures; he leads me to tranquil streams. —Ps 23:1-2

REFLECTION. In this life, we lack many things. The psalmist did as well. But he believed that God would eventually take care of his needs.

God has given us a down payment on this in Christ, the Good Shepherd. In Revelation, John says that in the coming kingdom Christ will guide God's faithful to springs of live-giving water. Then we'll lack nothing at all.

PRAYER. *O Lord, make me hungry and thirsty for Your company in the eternal kingdom.*

BESIDES you there is nothing else I desire on earth. Even should my heart and my flesh fail, God is the rock of my heart and my portion forever. —Ps 73:25b-26

NOV. 6

REFLECTION. To be holy is to be wholly devoted to the Lord, focused entirely on Him. This singleness of desire, or simplicity, is a characteristic shared by those whom the Church has recognized as saints.

The road to holiness or saintliness for us too lies in the elimination of competing desires and goals, or at the very least in making God our highest priority.

PRAYER. *Lord, make me holy as You are holy.*

WHEN I am terrified, I place my trust in you. In God, whose word I praise, in God I place my trust and know no fear; what can people do to me? —Ps 56:4-5

NOV. 7

REFLECTION. Others can hurt us, steal our property, damage our good name, cost us our livelihood, and rob us of health and life itself. They can hurt us in all these ways, but they cannot take from us our goodness and our eternal destiny.

God is stronger than our enemies. If we rely on Him to sustain our integrity when under attack, we shall be victorious like Jesus.

PRAYER. *Almighty God, fill me with Your courage and strength when I cry out to You.*

YOU will eat the fruit of your labors; you will enjoy both blessings and prosperity. —Ps 128:2

NOV. 8

REFLECTION. St. Paul observed that while we do the planting God provides the growth. "Your labors" indicates that we may not omit our part. And that God does His part is suggested by the element of promise in "you will."

Success is not automatic; it is not something we may presume. We must both work and pray for the Lord's blessing. If God withholds His blessing, He has good reasons for doing so.

PRAYER. *O Lord, grant success to our labors.*

 THERE is a river whose streams bring joy to the city of God, the holy place where the Most High dwells. —Ps 46:5

NOV. 9

REFLECTION. In the new Jerusalem there will be no Temple, for a stream of life-giving water shall flow from the divine throne of God and the Lamb.

Even now the Church or city of God has the life-giving water that flows from Jesus in Baptism and all the Sacraments: the Holy Spirit. We gather as the Church to celebrate the Sacraments and receive the Spirit.

PRAYER. *Almighty God, may the Spirit fill us with Your gifts and make us overflow with love.*

I F THE foundations are destroyed, what can be done by those who are righteous?

—Ps 11:3

NOV. 10

REFLECTION. Foundations are essential not only to buildings, but also to communities and to individuals. Jesus is the foundation for all Christian discipleship, but He also shares this function with St. Peter and his successors.

Jesus and the papacy often encounter opposition but will not be destroyed. Grateful for this, we must also attempt to stay connected to the foundation and to fellow Christians.

PRAYER. *Jesus, help me to appreciate my dependence on You and to stay connected every day.*

HE Lord makes a man's steps secure when he approves of his conduct. Even if he stumbles, he will never fall headlong, for the Lord holds him by the hand.

—Ps 37:23-24

NOV. 11

REFLECTION. Jesus fell under the weight of His Cross. There is no guarantee, then, that we shall not stumble and fall as we pursue holiness and try to do God's will.

But God holds us by the hand as a father his child. So our fall will not be headlong. And if we go down, we won't stay down.

PRAYER. *O God, hold me tight by Your grace which is abundant in Your Church.*

YOU must not bow down to an alien deity. I am the Lord, your God, who brought you up from the land of Egypt; open your mouth wide so that I may fill it. **NOV. 12** —Ps 81:10b-11

REFLECTION. Baby birds open wide their beaks to receive food from their mother. God tells Israel to expect the same from Him Who has freed them from Egyptian slavery.

God has made us His children and placed us in the bosom of the Church. There He does not fail to feed us with His word and the Sacraments, especially the Eucharist.

PRAYER. *Father, may we look to You for nourishment through the Church.*

 YOU provide grass for the cattle, and the plants for man to cultivate. You bring forth food from the earth and wine to gladden the heart of man, oil to make his face shine and bread to strengthen his body. **NOV. 13** —Ps 104:14-15

REFLECTION. Jesus observed that God provides well for the birds of the air and the lilies of the field, so that we should not question whether or not He will provide for us.

We need to honor by our care the plants and animals that God supplies, as He is the source of the bread, wine, oil, and all such things that nourish and delight us.

PRAYER. *Creator God, I praise You for Your extravagant gifts to us.*

LIFT up my eyes to you, to you who are enthroned in heaven. —Ps 123:1

REFLECTION. Because of differences in anatomy, human beings can look up more easily than animals can. This is not insignificant in God's design. Humans would never have gone to the moon if they had not been gazing at it forever.

We look beyond the moon and the stars to God in "the great beyond" because our true homeland is with Him there.

PRAYER. *Almighty God, keep my eyes and heart lifted in praise of You!*

 F A foe had treated me with contempt, I could manage to avoid him. But it was you, one like myself, a companion and a dear friend. —Ps 55:13b-14

REFLECTION. Because we are intimately close to our friends, we are also most vulnerable to them. When they turn against us, they hurt us more deeply than others. Jesus experienced just such treatment.

Jesus knew that this would happen all along, but He loved His friends anyway. The love of a dear friend is worth it even when it causes us pain.

PRAYER. *Lord Jesus, with You as my best friend, help me to risk reaching out to others.*

THE eyes of all look hopefully to you, and you give them their food at the right time. You open your hand and satisfy the needs of every living creature.
—Ps 145:15-16

NOV. 16

REFLECTION. Satisfying the needs of all creatures, including our own, depends on God. Our advanced knowledge of husbandry and agriculture helps us to cooperate better with God, but does not eliminate His action.

Our need to wait for the harvest shows us that we are not in ultimate control. This rests in the hands of God Who is not tight-fisted but extravagantly generous.

PRAYER. *Lord God, make me as generous as You in providing others with what they need.*

IN THE time of my distress I seek the Lord; at night I stretch out my hands unceasingly. . . . You keep my eyes from closing in sleep; I am much too distraught to speak.
—Ps 77:3a, 5

NOV. 17

REFLECTION. We can't sleep some nights because of our worries. God Himself has perpetual insomnia, for the psalmist tells us elsewhere that the Lord neither sleeps nor slumbers.

Rather than tossing or turning in bed or watching television, such nights may be the best time to connect with God in deep and protracted prayer.

PRAYER. *O God, answer my prayers and allow me to rest securely in You.*

OW lovely is your dwelling place, O Lord of hosts. My soul yearns and is filled with longing for the courts of the Lord. —Ps 84:2-3a

REFLECTION. Appropriately so, churches are beautifully decorated because they house Jesus in the Blessed Sacrament. Christians and the Church as a whole are lovelier still, because they are filled with the Holy Spirit.

A sure sign of the presence of the Spirit is our yearning for fellowship, a desire evident in St. Paul (Rom 1:11; Phil 1:8; 1 Thes 3:6).

PRAYER. *Lord, fill me with Your Spirit and increase my desire to be in Your household.*

 N THE Lord I take refuge. How can you say to me, "Flee like a bird to your mountains!" —Ps 11:1

REFLECTION. Jesus willingly went to the Garden to face His betrayer. He did not flee because He accepted God's will and He trusted that God would rescue Him.

We may be tempted to run when we realize that doing what God wants in a particular situation will bring us suffering. Then we need to recall Jesus' courage and God's faithfulness to Him.

PRAYER. *Father, may Your faithfulness to Your Son fill me with courage to do Your will.*

I LOVE you, O Lord, my strength, O Lord, **NOV.**
my rock, my fortress, my deliverer.
—Ps 18:2-3a **20**

REFLECTION. We are not used to a declaration of love like this, which is made by a believer in God. The psalmist can neither see nor touch God, but loves Him because he has experienced extraordinary freedom and protection.

Because we, too, are thus blessed, we should love God in turn with everything in us!

PRAYER. *O my God, may I love You with all my heart, soul, and strength.*

BLESSED are those who dwell in your **NOV.**
house; they offer continuous praise to
you. Blessed are those who find strength **21**
in you.
—Ps 84:5-6a

REFLECTION. We gather with friends at their homes or ours. Thus, we grow in friendship and are supported emotionally. For a similar reason God directed that the Israelites present themselves regularly in His house or Temple.

Christians grow in intimacy with God and derive joy and strength by being in His house, where Jesus is present in the Eucharist, His word, the assembly, and His ministers.

PRAYER. *O God, may we dwell with You in the gathering of Your holy people, the Church.*

HE Lord will fulfill his plan for me. Your kindness, O Lord, endures forever; do not forsake the work of your hands. —Ps 138:8

NOV. 22

REFLECTION. Like Adam, all of us are the work of God's hands. He shapes and molds us by the events and experiences of our lives, so that every one of us has a unique role in His plan.

God's plan for each of us is distinctive. With St. Paul, we may be confident that God will bring to fulfillment the good work He has begun in us.

PRAYER. *O Lord, help me to trust You and to be pliable clay in Your loving hands.*

 OW can I repay the Lord for all the good he has done for me? I will lift up the cup of salvation and call on the name of the Lord. —Ps 116:12-13

NOV. 23

REFLECTION. We cannot repay the Lord. He neither needs nor demands it because the good He does for us is done with the freedom that comes from love.

But if we respond to His love, God is greatly pleased and happy for us. In the celebration of the Eucharist, we join Jesus in His self-offering to the Father as an expression of our love and gratitude.

PRAYER. *All-loving God, grant me the grace to love You wholeheartedly.*

ET them give thanks to the Lord for his kindness and for the wonders he does for people. He has satisfied the thirsty and filled the hungry with good things.

—Ps 107:8-9

REFLECTION. If the earth did not yield a harvest, all humankind would be thirsty and hungry. Wherever there is a harvest, it is the result of more than human labors; it is a gift of God.

Gratitude to the Lord, which we should express always, is especially appropriate at harvest time, when His bounty is clearly in evidence.

PRAYER. *Almighty God, give me a grateful heart so that at all times I may glorify You with my whole being.*

 OME and listen, all you who fear God, while I relate what he has done for me.

—Ps 66:16

REFLECTION. To teach about God is to convey ideas about Him; it is an abstract affair. To proclaim God is to bear witness to Him; this is a matter of faith.

When we share how God has acted in our lives, then others are invited to recall and give witness to what God has done for them.

PRAYER. *Lord, help me to see what You have accomplished in my life and share it with others.*

THE Lord is enthroned forever; he has established his throne for judgment.

—Ps 9:8

NOV. 26

REFLECTION. A throne represents power. Earthly monarchs often exercise their power for their own advantage. God has set up His throne and He occupies it for others' advantage.

From the throne of His glory, Jesus will dispense justice, distinguishing between the righteous and the unrighteous according to the law of love.

PRAYER. *O Lord, may the certainty of future judgment help me to be just, fair, and loving in all my dealings with others.*

FOR judgment does not come from east or west, nor from the wilderness or the mountains. Rather, it is God who judges rightly, humbling one and exalting another.

— Ps 75:7-8

NOV. 27

REFLECTION. "It's not fair!" This complaint is frequently justified. But what will make things fair? Who will secure fairness for us? Other people? Social institutions?

Ultimately only God can and will ensure fairness for us because He alone judges rightly. When He does, the last may be first and the first last.

PRAYER. *Almighty God, as You judge rightly, help me also to discern what is just.*

RISE up, O Lord! Do not let man triumph; let the nations be judged before you. —Ps 9:20

REFLECTION. Without reference to God, humankind commits or permits gross injustice. The genocides of the twentieth century provide compelling proof.

But humankind has not prevailed and will not prevail in its injustice, for always God arises through righteous individuals to stem the tide of evil. And in the end, His justice will triumph everywhere.

PRAYER. *Lord God, may Your justice prevail so that all people may live in security and peace.*

LET them sing before the Lord, who is coming, coming to judge the earth. He will judge the world with justice and the nations with fairness. —Ps 98:9

REFLECTION. When judgment is just, then it results in fairness. Only God is perfectly just, and therefore only He is perfectly fair, because He does not judge by appearances but looks into the heart.

At His final coming, as at His first coming, the Lord Jesus will be supremely fair and enact perfect justice. This should be for us the cause of much joy.

PRAYER. *O Jesus, fill my heart with joy and put a song of praise on my lips.*

THEIR message goes forth throughout the earth, and their words to the ends of the world. —Ps 19:5a

REFLECTION. Jesus indicated that the Gospel would be preached to all nations before His return to start the new age.

Because God desires all to be saved, it is not enough that the message be taken to far-flung places but that it also be communicated where it has already arrived but not taken full hold.

PRAYER. *O Jesus, lacking a commission but believing in You, St. Andrew speedily told St. Peter about You. Help me to be an evangelizer.*

SHOUT to God with cries of gladness. For the Lord, the Most High, is awesome; he is the great King over all the earth. —Ps 47:2b-3

REFLECTION. God is indeed King over all the earth, but not everyone acknowledges His sovereignty. Sent to establish God's kingdom, Jesus is now subjugating every contrary power.

He Who was proclaimed King on the Cross is now seated at God's right hand. And as then, so also now, He extends God's sovereignty by mercy and love.

PRAYER. *Father, grant me Your grace to care for those in need, so that when Jesus sits on the throne of His glory, He may call me into Your kingdom.*

LESSED is he whose help is the God of Jacob, whose hope is in the Lord, his God. —Ps 146:5

REFLECTION. We count on others for help. Some come through for us; others do not. As well-intentioned as they may be, they cannot always do what we need.

Because the Lord came through for Jacob and his ancestors, He is worthy of our trust. We can and should count on Him for help, whatever the problems facing us might be.

PRAYER. *O Lord, God of Jacob, do not disappoint my trust in You, for You are my hope.*

OU are the hope of all the ends of the earth and of the far-off islands. —Ps 65:6b

REFLECTION. Initially, the Lord was the hope of Israel alone, but through Jesus He has become the hope of all peoples. The Lord gives all who believe in Him hope that they can love their neighbors and build a better society.

Hope in the Lord has been brought by missionaries even to far-off islands. Therefore, we are right to share our hope more locally, indeed within our family and immediate social circles.

PRAYER. *O Lord, make me a missionary to the people with whom I interact daily.*

THE needy will not be forgotten forever, nor will the hope of the afflicted ever come to naught. —Ps 9:19

DEC.
4

REFLECTION. God took notice of Israel's affliction in Egypt and eventually came to their rescue. Jesus noted the hunger of the crowds that followed Him and fed them miraculously and abundantly.

Because God cares, He will help those in need. Often God accomplishes this through ordinary means: us.

PRAYER. *O God, move me to assist the needy and suffering whose hopes may be withering.*

BEHOLD, as the eyes of servants are on the hand of their master, . . . so our eyes are on the Lord, our God, as we wait for him to show us his mercy. —Ps 123:2

DEC.
5

REFLECTION. When we require help from someone, we look in that person's direction and indeed into that person's eyes. We make contact.

We make contact with the Lord by adoring Him in the Blessed Sacrament and by every heartfelt prayer. God will give us the help we need and seek from Him.

PRAYER. *O Lord, move me to look to You in eager anticipation of Your help.*

THE future bodes well for him who is generous in helping those in need. **DEC. 6**

—Ps 112:5a

REFLECTION. Our usual approach to securing the future is to accumulate and store our resources. But this is a poor method, as Jesus' parable of the rich fool shows.

A better future is secured by sharing our resources with those in need. By this method, we store up for ourselves lasting treasure in heaven.

PRAYER. *O God, grant me the grace to be generous in sharing my resources.*

SING out your joy to God our strength; shout aloud to the God of Jacob. Raise the chant and sound the tambourine; play the pleasant harp and the lyre. **DEC. 7**

—Ps 81:2-3

REFLECTION. We sing when we are happy. A lover sings when he has found his beloved. Sports fans shout for all to hear when their team has won.

When Christians sing on joyous occasions, they name God because He is the source of all the good things that bring them joy.

PRAYER. *Almighty God, You are my strength and my song. I rejoice in Your blessings.*

E CHOSE the tribe of Judah, Mount Zion, which he loved. —Ps 78:68

REFLECTION. God chose the smallest of nations and one of its less significant tribes. He chose a low mountain for His Temple, and the youngest son as king of His people. Whomever God chooses, He then makes great by His gifts.

This is preeminently demonstrated in Mary whom God exempted from the stain of original sin so that she might be the Mother of His sinless Son. Mary embraced God's choice and gift.

PRAYER. *O God, help me to embrace the gifts You have chosen to give to me.*

 TIR up your power and come to save us. . . . Let your face shine upon us, and we will be saved. —Ps 80:3b, 4b

REFLECTION. There is no question of whether or not the Lord can rescue us, for to Him all things are possible.

Rather, the question is whether or not we will call out to Him in humility and ask Him to look upon us favorably. If we muster true humility, God will surely be pleased and stir up His power on our behalf.

PRAYER. *Almighty God, grant me the humility to know and admit my need of You in fervent prayer and petition.*

HOW long, O Lord—will you forget me forever? How long will you hide your face from me? —Ps 13:2

REFLECTION. Young children everywhere love to play peek-a-boo. They are testing and relishing the notion that even though something cannot be seen at the moment, it is still present and will eventually appear.

The psalmist, like the little child, is eager for God to put in an appearance. Therefore, he asks how long it will be before He does so.

PRAYER. *O Lord, grant me the certainty that You will help me, even if I must wait.*

MAKE haste, O God, to rescue me; O Lord, come quickly to my aid. —Ps 70:2

REFLECTION. God's help is not superfluous. It is not "an extra" for good measure. No, God's help is critical, even if it often goes unnoticed, because it undergirds all human efforts and makes them effective.

This is why it is appropriate to beseech the Lord with a sense of urgency.

PRAYER. *O God, because Your help is essential, do not delay in giving it, and help me to recognize it when it comes.*

HE WHO pours forth his contempt on princes makes them wander in track-less wastes, while he raises the needy from their misery. —Ps 107:40-41a

DEC. 12

REFLECTION. "The first will be last, and the last will be first." The first ought not to be proud, and the last ought not to despise themselves.

Because God is just, He will humble the proud and exalt the lowly—so Mary declared in her *Magnificat*. And our Lady has made herself the instrument of such "divine reversal" by choosing to make her apparitions to those considered insignificant.

PRAYER. *O Mary, look upon my lowliness, and ask God to take me out of my sadness.*

BUT the eyes of the Lord are on those who fear him, on those who trust in his kindness, to deliver them from death. —Ps 33:18-19a

DEC. 13

REFLECTION. It is said that St. Lucy had such beautiful eyes that others would gaze at her. But her own eyes were on the Lord. Like God's faithful people in the Bible, she found favor in God's eyes.

What draws our attention and notice? We should have eyes for those in need with whom Jesus identified Himself.

PRAYER. *Almighty God, help me to keep my eyes fixed on Jesus and the marginalized.*

AIT quietly for the Lord and be patient until he comes. Do not fret over the man who prospers because of his evil schemes.

—Ps 37:7

14

REFLECTION. We are easily unnerved by evil's success, as though God might have missed it or doesn't care. He cares and wants to see if we care as much as He does. Then He will act.

Many of us have difficulty being patient when evil abounds. According to St. Paul, patience is a characteristic of love (1 Cor 13:4).

PRAYER. *O Lord, fill me with the kind of love for You that is willing to suffer and wait for Your intervention.*

LACE your hope in the Lord: be strong and courageous in your heart, and place your hope in the Lord.   —Ps 27:14

DEC.
15

REFLECTION. Many people project a bright future on the basis of their abilities and past successes. But when one has seen the limits of one's abilities and witnessed past successes vanish like smoke, then one is less inclined to bank on oneself.

It is the Lord Who fulfills any of our hopes along life's journey, and His gracious help is the real basis of our hopes for the future.

PRAYER. *Father, give me the courage and strength that come with hope in You.*

UR God is coming, and he will not be silent. —Ps 50:3a

DEC.
16

REFLECTION. There is a time for everything. There is a time to be silent and a time to speak. When He became flesh, God the Son spoke. When He returns, He will again speak in order to call to Himself the righteous according to the standard of the Gospel.

Our God is coming! We prepare for His second coming by celebrating His first coming and listening to His word.

PRAYER. *O Word Made Flesh, teach me when to be silent and when to speak.*

 USTICE will reign in his days, and peace will abound until the moon is no more. —Ps 72:7

DEC.
17

REFLECTION. Isaiah prophesied that God's Servant would bring justice to the nations, but not by strife or violence.

Rather, it would be by means of teaching and healing. Peace abounds in the lives of those who follow Jesus, God's Servant, in securing justice.

PRAYER. *O God, until the time when the moon will no longer give its light at the dawn of the new creation, make us instruments of peace by filling us with Your kindness.*

E WILL have pity on the lowly and the poor; the lives of the needy he will save. —Ps 72:13

REFLECTION. The psalmist expressed the hope that the king chosen and graced by God would treat the lowly with compassion and save the needy.

It was as the expression of God's compassion that Jesus was begotten in the womb of the Blessed Virgin Mary so as to reign over God's people without end.

PRAYER. *Father, I thank You for giving us the promised King, Jesus, Who takes note of our lowliness and treats us with pity on the way to salvation.*

 WILL speak of your mighty deeds, O Lord God, and declare your righteousness, yours alone. O God, you have taught me from my youth, and to this day I proclaim your marvelous works. —Ps 71:16-17

REFLECTION. During the time that God did not grant a child to Elizabeth and Zachary, it may have seemed that He was not doing right by them.

But God proved otherwise when He rewarded their faith and patience by John's birth. In turn, they trained John to trust God totally.

PRAYER. *O Lord, when I am frustrated, help me to trust in You and to wait patiently.*

HO may ascend the mountain of the Lord? Who may stand in his holy place? One who has clean hands and a pure heart, who does not turn his mind to vanities.

DEC.
20

—Ps 24:3-4a

REFLECTION. Mountain climbers reach the summit by skill and training, but primarily by focus. If we would reach God, we must do the right thing and have the right intention, but first of all we must focus.

We may not allow ourselves the luxury of entertaining distractions or pursuing vanities; rather, we must desire and seek God.

PRAYER. *O God, Mary set aside her plans when You made clear to her Your plans. Help us to be equally focused and trusting.*

 UR soul waits in hope for the Lord; he is our help and our shield. Our hearts rejoice in him because we trust in his holy name. —Ps 33:20-21

DEC.
21

REFLECTION. Israel waited for the fulfillment of God's promise of the Messiah. As a daughter of Israel, the Blessed Virgin Mary shared this hope.

Indeed, she took it personally; for, as Elizabeth observed, Mary believed that God's word to her would be fulfilled. And how personally God fulfilled His promise by choosing her to be the Messiah's Mother!

PRAYER. *Lord, help me to see in Your promises to Your people a place also for me.*

E SETTLES the barren woman in a home and makes her the joyful mother of children.
—Ps 113:9

DEC. 22

REFLECTION. The inability to have children is a cause of great suffering to married couples. God famously reversed this situation for Sarah, Hannah, and Elizabeth.

Then God enabled even a virgin, Mary of Nazareth, to conceive and give birth without male intervention. Miracles happen.

PRAYER. *Almighty God, to You all things are possible. Look kindly upon all infertile couples, grant them the miracle for which they pray, and let them find joy in You.*

 AKE your ways known to me, O Lord; teach me your paths. Guide me in your truth and instruct me, for you are God, my Savior.
—Ps 25:4-5a

DEC. 23

REFLECTION. "Ways" and "paths" imply a journey—a starting point and a destination. The whole world and all of us in it have God as our origin and destiny.

Because God wants to save us from dangers on our journey, He seeks to instruct and guide us through Jesus and the Church.

PRAYER. *O God, as I rely on my GPS, I depend on Your guidance. Help me to seek it out every day and grant it to me in abundance.*

E WILL cry to me, "You are my Father, my God, the Rock of my salvation." . . . My covenant with him will never end. —Ps 89:27, 29b

DEC. 24

REFLECTION. The royal heir to David's throne was to look upon the Lord not only as God and Savior, but also as Father.

God promised to give to Jesus "the throne of David, his father," and Jesus would eventually call upon God as Father and reveal Him completely to us as God's own Incarnate Son.

PRAYER. *Lord God, because Jesus has invited us into the relationship He has with You, grant us to live this covenant in the power of the Holy Spirit.*

HE Lord has made known his salvation; he has manifested his righteousness for all the nations to see. —Ps 98:2

DEC. 25

REFLECTION. As John put it, "God so loved the world that he gave his only Son, so that everyone who believes in him might not perish but might have eternal life."

The Incarnation of the Eternal Son is God's way of demonstrating His love and inspiring our trust in Him, which is vital to our being saved.

PRAYER. *Heavenly Father, grant us the grace to grasp the hand You have stretched out to us and to hold on to Jesus with faith wherever He may daily direct us.*

ET your face shine upon your servant; save me in your kindness. —Ps 31:17

DEC.
26

REFLECTION. By becoming man in Jesus, God acquired a human face that shone with unadulterated love upon all men and women, so that their own faces might ultimately shine with angelic love even upon their enemies.

The Son of God became human so that human beings might have a share in divine nature.

PRAYER. *Almighty God, as You transformed St. Stephen into a shining image of Jesus, so transform me by the grace of the Holy Spirit into a convincing witness of Your Son.*

IGHT dawns for the righteous, and joy for the upright of heart. —Ps 97:11

DEC.
27

REFLECTION. Referring to God's Son or Word, St. John wrote that the true Light came into the world to enlighten everyone, yet not all came near the Light. Those who did evil avoided the Light lest their deeds be exposed.

If we do not yet have the righteousness of good deeds, by faith God can eventually get us there and save us.

PRAYER. *O God, grant me the faith to believe that You will help me to overcome whatever sins may come to light as I draw closer to Jesus.*

UR help is in the name of the Lord, the Maker of heaven and earth.

—Ps 124:8

DEC. 28

REFLECTION. When the innocent suffer, people of faith are certain that God will save them nonetheless; for God Who made everything to exist out of nothing will certainly right wrongs in His good time and restore us finally to a fuller life.

We cannot imagine ourselves to be helpless, when our helper is the Creator Himself.

PRAYER. *Lord, grant me never to despair even in the face of grave injustice and harm, but to cry out to You as Jesus did.*

 ING to the Lord and bless his name; proclaim his salvation day after day.

—Ps 96:2

DEC. 29

REFLECTION. The events surrounding Jesus' birth caused God's faithful to break out in hymns of praise: Mary's *Magnificat*, Zachary's *Benedictus*, the Angels' *Gloria*, and Simeon's *Nunc Dimittis*.

As Simeon held Jesus, he proclaimed that he was seeing God's salvation, and so had come to his life's finale. At the end, the saints will sing of God's salvation through Christ.

PRAYER. *Almighty God, because I want ultimately to sing Your praises in Your kingdom, help me even now to praise You.*

LESSED are all those who fear the Lord and walk in his ways. —Ps 128:1

REFLECTION. Families that revere the Lord and live according to His word will be blessed. These blessings may be natural, such as prosperity, but also spiritual, such as harmony.

No faithful family is without its blessings from God; at the same time, it may not escape difficulties and even opposition. But God will defend the Christian family as He did the Holy Family.

PRAYER. *O God, help us to wait for Your blessings whenever we are experiencing loss or sorrow.*

 ET all the trees of the forest shout for joy before the Lord, for he is coming, coming to judge the earth. He will judge the world with justice. —Ps 96:12b-13a

REFLECTION. At the end of the current age, the Lord will come and sit in judgment on the entire world. He will distinguish between the wicked and the righteous, the selfish and the loving.

It will be a time of joy for those to whom Jesus says, "Come, you who are blessed by my Father. Inherit the kingdom prepared for you from the foundation of the world."

PRAYER. *Almighty God, as time marches on, help me to stay focused on the only ending that matters.*

HOLY WEEK

HOLY THURSDAY

E DIVIDED the sea so that they could pass. —Ps 78:13a

REFLECTION. "Before the feast of the Passover, when Jesus knew that his hour had come to pass from this world to the Father, having loved his own who were in the world, he loved them to the end."

The proof that we ourselves have passed from ordinary life to a fuller life is our love for others.

PRAYER. *Jesus, when I am afraid of loving for fear of losing my life, give me faith and courage.*

GOOD FRIDAY

NTO your hands I commend my spirit; you will redeem me, O Lord, God of truth. —Ps 31:6

REFLECTION. As He was dying, Jesus entrusted Himself to God in the confident hope that He would restore Him to life. God would do precisely this on Easter Sunday.

Because the risen Jesus took His place at the Father's side, St. Stephen confidently called on Jesus and entrusted himself to Him as he faced execution (Acts 7:59).

PRAYER. *Father, help us to accept our problems and suffering with confident faith.*

HOLY SATURDAY

Y SOUL rejoices; my body too is filled with confidence, for you will not abandon me to the netherworld.

—Ps 16:9b-10a

REFLECTION. Jesus was put into the tomb, and He remained there until Easter Sunday when He left the netherworld.

While He may have felt abandoned on the Cross, He was sure that God would not in fact desert Him. He was confident of it, and God did not disappoint Him.

PRAYER. *O God, in the face of death fill me with faith that You will not leave me in the grave.*

EASTER SUNDAY

HE right hand of the Lord is exalted. . . . I shall not die; rather I shall live and recount the works of the Lord.

—Ps 118:16a, 17

REFLECTION. Those who are very ill sometimes escape death but they do not die and come back to life to live more fully. Yet Jesus died and rose to eternal life.

Although doctors may keep sick people from dying, Jesus' resurrection is about what only God could accomplish. St. Peter said, "By his right hand God has raised him up to be leader and savior."

PRAYER. *Father, help me to believe that You will raise me up to eternal life.*

Prayer for God's Living Word

BLESSED are You, Lord God,
King of the Universe,
for giving us Your living word in the Scriptures
that we may be fully competent
and equipped for every good work.
Your word is living and effective,
sharper than any two-edged sword;
it judges the thoughts of our heart,
and endures forever.

By the light of faith
and by meditation on Your word,
may we always and everywhere recognize You
in Whom we live and move and have our being,
seek Your will in every event,
see Christ in all human beings,
and make correct judgments
about the true meaning and value of temporal
   things
both in themselves and in their relation to our
   final good.

OTHER OUTSTANDING CATHOLIC BOOKS

THE PSALMS—New Catholic Version—A new translation of the Book of Psalms of the Old Testament, which is often termed the "Gospel of the Holy Spirit." Printed in large easy-to-read type with informative notes and cross-references. **No. 665**

NEW TESTAMENT AND PSALMS-New Catholic Version—This contemporary translation features readable, insightful, and informative footnotes; helpful cross-references; 36 two-color illustrations; and the words of Christ in red. **No. 647**

THE IMITATION OF CHRIST—Zipper Binding. By Thomas à Kempis. The one religious book that is second only to the Bible in popularity. It shows readers how to follow the life of Christ and includes a full color Rosary and Stations of the Cross section. **No. 320/23BG**

CONFESSIONS OF ST. AUGUSTINE—New translation of the Christian classic that—after the Bible and the Imitation of Christ—is the most widely translated and the most universally esteemed. It is published in prayer book format as befits its nature. **No. 173**

INTRODUCTION TO A DEVOUT LIFE—Adapted by Sr. Halcon J. Fisk. St. Francis de Sales known as the apostle of love, reached out to everyone through this small book. showing that devotion is available to everyone in every walk of life and occupation. **No. 163**

MARY DAY BY DAY—Minute meditations for every day of the year, including a Scripture passage, a quotation from the Saints, and a concluding prayer. Printed in two colors with over 300 illustrations. **No. 180**

ST. JOSEPH BIBLE HANDBOOK—An indispensable guide to opening up every book of the Old and New Testaments of the Bible—for schools, Bible study groups, and personal use. **No. 649**

BIBLE DAY BY DAY—By Rev. John Kersten, S.V.D. Minute Bible meditations for every day including a short Scripture text and brief reflection. Printed in two colors with 300 illustrations. **No. 150**

MINUTE MEDITATIONS FOR EACH DAY— By Rev. Bede Naegele O.C.D. This very attractive book offers a short Scripture text, a practical reflection, and a meaningful prayer for each day of the year. **No. 190**

www.catholicbookpublishing.com

ISBN 978-1-941243-05-3

90000

9 781941 243053